Jubilee
GOD'S GOOD NEWS

Teacher's Guide
Middler
Cycle A, Spring

Jesus' Advice for Action

Written by June Galle Krehbiel

Brethren Press
Elgin, Illinois 60120

Evangel Publishing House
Nappanee, Indiana 46550

Faith & Life Press
Newton, Kansas 67114

Mennonite Publishing House
Scottdale, Pennsylvania 15683

Contents

●●●

Jesus' Advice for Action

Jubilee: God's Good News

Jesus' Advice for Action: is the Middler, Cycle A, Spring curriculum for grades 3, 4, and 5 in Jubilee: God's Good News.

Jubilee: God's Good News is published by the Brethren in Christ Church, the Church of the Brethren, the General Conference Mennonite Church, and the Mennonite Church. Supporting denominations: Friends United Meeting and the Mennonite Brethren Church. Executive Director, Rosella Wiens Regier. Editors: Glen A. Pierce, Brethren in Christ Church; Julie Garber, Church of the Brethren; Elizabeth Raid Pankratz, General Conference Mennonite Church; Marjorie Waybill, Mennonite Church. Project Designer, Merrill R. Miller. Bible Outlines and Consultant, Ronald D. Guengerich. Education Consultant, Sandra E. Schiedel. Early Childhood Bible Outlines and Consultant, Betta Kym.

Jesus' Advice for Action: Writer, June Galle Krehbiel. Illustrator, Ray Dirks. Cover illustration, *Jesus on the Cross,* by Joy Dunn Keenan.

Jubilee: God's Good News
Introduction

• •

You said yes to God, to the children, and to your congregation to teach a quarter of materials from the curriculum **Jubilee: God's Good News.** You committed yourself to this ministry, and now you are about to begin!

Teaching children is holy work. In the midst of the congregation, you will help children learn to know and love Jesus and to follow him. Enjoy the children. Love them, learn from them and with them. Plan well and try new things. Together with God, you will help nurture children toward mature Christian faith.

This Is Jubilee

Jubilee: God's Good News is a children's curriculum that invites children and adults through the biblical story to follow Jesus, to learn and grow together, and to discover the power of the Holy Spirit to form faith, inform minds, and transform lives.

Children will be introduced to stories in the Old and New Testaments of the Bible. You will **invite** children to experience the good news of Jesus, to follow him, and to **celebrate** the richness of the biblical message of **Jubilee**: God's gift of reconciliation and justice to all.

Frame your teaching with this message of grace and hope found in Jesus' words: "The Spirit of the Lord is upon me, because he has anointed me to bring good news to the poor. He has sent me to proclaim release to the captives and recovery of sight to the blind, to let the oppressed go free, to proclaim the year of the Lord's favor" (Luke 4:18-19, NRSV).

The Jubilee Plan

Jubilee is a three-year plan: Cycles A, B, C. Children will move through the three cycles, then go on to the next level. Each year is divided into four quarters with thirteen sessions each. There are materials for four age-groups. Each age-group works from the same biblical material:

Early Childhood (ages 2, 3, and 4)
Primary (kindergarten and grades 1 and 2)
Middler (grades 3, 4, and 5)
Junior Youth (grades 6, 7, and 8)

Summer in Jubilee. In the summer, Early Childhood has its own plan, as in the other quarters. Primary, Middler, and Junior Youth levels study the same Scripture text. Churches may conduct separate age-group classes or combine for broadly graded experiences.

Parallel Studies. During Advent, at Easter, in the summertime, and during Cycle C winter and spring quarters, children from kindergarten to grade 8 all study the same Bible passages during the same sessions. Classes may work in their own rooms, or the plan also offers possibilities to combine groups for wide-age-range learning.

Flexible Class Groupings. Jubilee materials let **you** choose how to organize for Sunday school classes. Which way fits your church best?

1. Three grades together. Three ages learn together. A good plan for small churches and for those who intentionally combine ages.

2. Single ages or grades. The material is designed for the three ages listed and also works well for single-age classes. The Teacher's Guide gives ideas for teaching specific ages.

3. Combination of two-grade and one-grade classes. Perhaps space or numbers of children will lead you to this combination.

4. Classes with more than three grades together. Since all levels have ideas to fit many abilities, you may combine many grades.

Jubilee Celebration Events. Jubilee: God's Good News is a curriculum for the whole church, both in the classroom and in encounters with the entire congregation. In a separate book called *Jubilee Celebrations* you will find plans for churchwide events that supplement the classroom education program in **Jubilee.** *Jubilee Celebrations* features eight two-hour programs for worship and education that involve the whole church on Sunday mornings or any other time. Notes in the margins and on the inside back cover of this Teacher's Guide help you plan these celebrations with other teachers and the worship committee of your church.

The Jubilee Materials

Each **Jubilee** quarter has four parts:
•**Teacher's Guide.** A step-by-step guide for thirteen sessions. Features include this Introduction, editor's and writer's pages, and a resource section.
•**Student Pack.** Materials for children to use in the session and at home.
•**Resource Box.** Special items that are vital to teaching the sessions and to the classroom environment.
•**General Classroom Items.** Essential one-time purchase items.

A Jubilee Session

Every session in **Jubilee** follows the same basic plan. Material is provided for sixty-minute sessions. Worship and music are included in each session so larger group openings are not needed.

•**Teacher Preparation.** Meditation, supplies, and preparations.
•**Bible Study for Teacher Enrichment.** Helpful background Bible study and insights about children and Scripture.
•**Student Experience.** A core session in four parts: Beginning Moments, Bible Story, Responses to the Bible Story, and Closing Moments.
•**Choices.** Other ways to respond to the story provide a large selection of ideas from which to choose. Match choices to class needs.
•**Teaching Ideas for Specific Ages.** Ideas to understand ages developmentally, variations about session process, and new ideas precisely for one age.
•**Teaching Tip.** Hints to teach the session: insights about children, the creative processes, classroom management, and more.
•**Memory Work.** Various ways to challenge children to commit Scriptures to memory.

Don't miss this!

Jubilee and the Teaching Environment

Try to arrange your classroom with two areas: a work space (usually a table with chairs) and an open story and discussion area. This encourages movement for active learning. Create a bulletin board on one full wall (top to bottom) to feature children's work and quarter activities. Another full wall with open shelves gives easy access to Bibles, materials, supplies, learning centers, a worship center, and more, without taking room space.

Jubilee and the Bible

Bible Translations. Recommended Scripture translations are the New Revised Standard Version (NRSV) and the New International Version (NIV).

Bible Focus. Each session in **Jubilee** focuses on a biblical passage: Old Testament stories told in chronological order in the fall quarter, and stories from the Gospels and the life of Jesus in winter and spring quarters to correspond naturally to the Christmas and Easter seasons. Summers follow a new theme each year.

Bible Perspectives. You as a teacher will introduce children to God who brings newness, freshness, and change. You will share a story that turns us around. Children will hear Bible stories about people who have physical, social, and spiritual needs—needs that are met by a God of grace and by people with human faces. Children will feel and share the plight of others and are encouraged to help at the level of their own abilities.

Bible Framework. Younger children learn through the simple telling of the story: they are **formed.** Middler children are **informed** by the wisdom of the gathered community. As Junior Youth mature, they are **transformed** by the power of the Holy Spirit working through teachers, people in the Bible who made radical commitments, the children's caregivers, and role models in the congregation.

Bible Story Approach. The Bible story is the basis of **Jubilee** and of each session. Children will see themselves and Bible characters through eyes open to issues of need and justice. Together, you will think about right relationships with others and with God. You will all learn that God does new and surprising things in their lives and in our world.

Beliefs and Teachings Central to Jubilee

Here are basic beliefs held by Anabaptists and Quakers and taught in **Jubilee:**

- God exists and relates to us.
- Jesus Christ is Savior of the world.
- The Holy Spirit assures and empowers us.
- Salvation is a personal, redemptive experience in Jesus Christ that is encouraged in the Christian community, the congregation.
- The Bible and the Holy Spirit are our guides for faith and life.
- Responses to Jesus Christ need to be appropriate for a child's age.
- Believer's baptism is an inward baptism of the Holy Spirit and an outward baptism of water by the congregation.
- Discipleship means to live a life following Christ.
- Peacemaking is a core component of our beliefs.
- Simple lifestyles grow out of Jesus' teachings.
- All peoples, races, and sexes are valued in God's family.
- Community and cooperation are emphasized in the congregation.
- Service and worldwide mission grow out of active discipleship.

• Worship is both a celebration of God's activity in our lives and an occasion to renew our commitment to God.

Children and Faith Experiences

In **Jubilee** little children are taught that they are loved by God and are safe and secure with God. Jesus said: "Let the little children come to me, and do not stop them; for it is to such as these that the kingdom of heaven belongs" (Matthew 19:14, NRSV). However, all eventually fall short of the mark and need the grace and forgiveness of God in their lives.

Jubilee takes the gospel seriously and believes that as the story is faithfully told by teachers and the congregation, children will hear the call of God to commit their lives to Jesus Christ. For some, dramatic conversion events will be experienced; others respond to God like a flower opening to the rays of sunlight. We cannot know precisely how God will work through the Holy Spirit in our lives. We simply believe "faith comes from hearing the message, and the message is heard through the word of Christ" (Romans 10:17, NIV).

Storytelling and Wondering in Jubilee

Storytelling. Telling the stories of the Bible is at the heart of each **Jubilee** session. Two primary methods are featured:
• Bible storytelling with the Spiral Teaching Picture Book.
• Bible storytelling with Story Figures. Junior Youth materials include storytelling and also Bible study techniques.

Tell the Bible story with the Spiral Teaching Picture Book:
• Hold an open Bible in your lap.
• Place the spiral book comfortably beside you, or at a worship center or table.

• Tell the story or read it well.
• Maintain eye contact with the children.
• Point to the picture as you talk.

Tell the Bible story with Story Figures:
• The story begins when you reach for or get the Story Figures from the shelves.
• Make all movements deliberate: carefully define the space; smooth a bath towel, construction paper, or wood piece on a table or floor space.
• Gently pick up a figure from the edge of the story space, and set it in place as you begin telling the story.
• Concentrate on the figures as you tell the story, though at times you may prefer eye contact with the children.
• Decide ahead of time, as you prepare the story, when and where the figures will move to help tell the story.
• Leave the figures in place for the wondering questions.
• At the end, return them carefully to their box or leave them in place for the Bible story responses.

Wondering. The moments immediately following the Bible story—whether you use the Spiral Teaching Picture Book or the Story Figures—are a time for children to reflect and meditate. Formulate questions that lead children to internalize meaning and to seek direction together with their class group.
• Ask questions in which you muse, to which you do not expect oral answers. Children think quietly; they listen to the voice of God and to their own inner feelings and longings.
• Ask questions that encourage group interaction: one-word thoughts, their own questions, discussion with others.

Teaching Approaches in Jubilee

• **Experiential Learning. Jubilee** encourages an active approach to learning: storytelling, music, art, drama, sharing, wondering, writing, movement, research, decision making, discussion.

•**Choices.** In **Jubilee,** you as teachers will make choices for the teaching plan. There are total group, smaller group, and individual experiences. Children are also encouraged to make choices when responding to the Bible story. The time provided for children to select an activity of their choice is important for young children as they learn to live and relate. Making choices about ways to learn helps make learning meaningful, fun, and enriching.

•**Developmentally based.** Session activities have been carefully chosen to relate to the developmental abilities of children of each age-group.

•**Abilities, Interests, and Learning Styles.** Children have different abilities, varied interests, and learn in different ways. There can be as much difference among children in one age-group as among several grades of children. **Jubilee** recognizes those differences by giving choices, varying methods, and offering a range of activities to meet the needs of children.

Classroom Management

Everyone learns best in an atmosphere of love and trust, where there is respect for people and materials. Teachers set the tone for learning. Show quiet confidence, purpose, energy, and direction. Children get their cues from you. Define the learning atmosphere. Help children understand it and abide by it.

1. Be consistent about your expectations.

2. Appeal to individual children privately.

3. Involve the children to help to set up guidelines based on need.

4. Follow the agreed-upon guidelines. Define the consequences.

5. Invite others—superintendents, parents, caring adults—to help create a positive learning atmosphere.

Home Connections

Jubilee curriculum acknowledges that the home can be one of the strongest settings for the Christian nurture of children. **Jubilee** is committed to assisting caregivers with that task through a strong Sunday school program and by extending the curriculum to the home experience of each child. Each quarter of sessions features unique ways to connect the child, the home, and the Sunday school experience:

•weekly messages in the Student Pack to caregivers

•quarterly letters to parents

•suggestions for adults in the home to expand on the session experience through discussion or activity.

To help encourage interaction at home, parts of the Student Activity Book or the Student Leaflet may be completed at home instead of during the session.

Jubilee Quarter Evaluation: What Do You Think?

When you have completed teaching a quarter of sessions, please share your experiences, affirmations, and concerns with **Jubilee** planners. Copy the form (on the last page of the Teacher's Guide) "What Do You Think?" complete it, and mail it to the address listed on the form.

●●

EDITOR'S PAGE

June Galle Krehbiel

Welcome!

Welcome to an exciting adventure teaching middler children and learning together about Jesus and his advice for living. The lessons this quarter are taken from Luke 11—24. The memory passage is Luke 12:22-31. Try to memorize this passage together with the children. Your example will encourage them, and you may be surprised how much you learn from them.

Meet the Writer

June Galle Krehbiel lives in Moundridge, Kansas, where she is a member of Eden Mennonite Church. She has taught Sunday school for various ages—second grade through adult. June has been a public school teacher and served with her husband, Perry, in Nigeria as a teacher under Mennonite Central Committee. Writing is her chosen vocation. Her byline appears occasionally in Mennonite publications. She likes music, reading, and gardening. June and Perry are the parents of two children, Melanie and Joel.

Meet the Consultants

A team of people from June's congregation served as consultants. They met weekly to generate, review, and respond to ideas and offer encouragement and support. This team included Donna Goering, Lillie Goering, Donovan R. Graber, and Marcella Schrag.

Use the Materials

1. This **Teacher's Guide** is designed to make your teaching effective. The Teacher Preparation and Bible Study for Teacher Enrichment sections help you prepare. The Student Experience section contains the complete session plan. Follow it step-by-step as you teach. The Bible Story is boxed for easy reference. The same story also appears in the Spiral Teaching Picture Book.

Use the additional activities in the Choices section to vary the basic session plan. Choose activities that will work with your group of children. The Teaching Grade Three, Teaching Grade Four, and Teaching Grade Five sections give specific ideas to make the basic session plan work for each grade level.

2. The **Resource Box** contains a cassette, a Sectional Time Line, a Bible Memory Poster, an ACTS Game, a Jerusalem Map, a Lenten Candle Cross Mat, a Song Chart, and Session Helps. Use these items to enrich your teaching and the children's learning. The Teacher's Guide gives directions for ways to use these items each session.

Some of the stories in the Teacher's Guide contain movements for the story figures. Story figures are an essential one-time purchase. They should be kept in the classroom and used each quarter.

3. The **Student Pack** contains a four-page Student Leaflet that each child should receive every week. The Jerusalem Moments Calendar should be given to each child at the beginning of the quarter. This calendar has daily devotions and activities for the child to do. Use these student items to make a connection with the home. The Teacher's Guide gives more ideas for use of these student pieces in class and at home.

Good News

June has seen her Jubilee writing as holy work. She has given joyfully of her time and talents to create these materials. She has prayed, worked, tested, written, and rewritten to make these sessions come alive for you as a teacher and for the children you teach. Her creative flair for hands-on and interactive learning provide exciting activities that reinforce the session themes and meet the different learning styles of children.

May you experience God's leading and blessing in your life as you teach and learn from Jesus' advise for action.

Plant a Garden in Your Classroom
(and other inspiration as you begin the quarter)

Every spring our family plants a garden. We stick tiny vegetable seeds into newly turned soil and wait for our garden to appear. Teaching Sunday school is like planting a garden. As you teach these Luke lessons, I ask you to think of your children as young garden plants. Some of them will develop as expected. Others will require patience as they explore many options before finding an activity that grabs their attention. Some children may never bloom in the classroom, but later on—perhaps years later—you will discover how your teaching shaped their lives.

Prepare yourself just as a gardener would prepare for spring planting. Read the sessions. Mark important items. Collect supplies. Study the stories. Search for media resources. Make plans for a service project.

Schedule Session 3 for Easter Sunday. Sessions 1 and 2 immediately precede Easter. Session 4 follows Easter Sunday. The other sessions are intended to be used in order. If you must skip one or two sessions, choose to eliminate sessions with Bible texts that children know well.

Get a helper. If you are a seasoned teacher, enlist the help of an inexperienced volunteer. If you are a first-timer, seek a helper who has classroom experience or who knows the children well.

Learn the stories. Without them the sessions will lose their zest. Train yourself in the art of storytelling. Focus on telling the story rather than reading it. Memorize only the main points. Then lay aside the script and make the story your own. Become one of the characters. Imagine what it was like to walk with Jesus. Make the story important to you, and it will become important to the children.

Prepare your room. Even though the appearance of the classroom may not be important to you, it will seem very important to the children. Make the room as inviting as possible. Decorate the door, bulletin board, or wall with one of the ideas on pages 88-89.

Set up a worship center in a quiet corner. On a low table place the Lenten Candle Cross Mat from the Resource Box, an open Bible, the Spiral Teaching Picture Book, and a few flowers. On a floor mat place the box with the story figures. Sit near the low table and the story figures. The children can sit on the floor. Before you begin the story, open the Bible to the text. Help the children make the connection between God's word and the story you will tell.

Provide a worktable that is large enough for all children to sit or stand beside it while they complete writing or art projects. A folding table is ideal so that it can be moved when activities demand space.

Focus on the children. Send a letter to all children inviting them to share the quarter with you. Explain the format for offerings and Bible memory. Tell them about any special projects.

Plan to arrive before the children come. Greet all the children warmly. Engage them in the Beginning Moments of the session. Capture them with a well-told story. Let them respond as they choose and send them away with Student Leaflets that will remind them all week of their Jubilee experience.

Plant your classroom garden well. Nurture it. Water it. Care for it, and don't be surprised if you discover lilies blooming where you last saw thistles.

The Lord's Supper

TEACHER PREPARATION

Recipe for Golan Discs (unleavened bread): *Combine 2 cups flour and ¹/₂ teaspoon salt. Add water (approx. ³/₄ cup) to make a dough that will clean the sides of the bowl and can be gathered into a ball. Turn out onto lightly floured board and knead 10 minutes. Cut and roll into 8 balls. Roll out each ball to form a 7-inch circle. Bake on ungreased baking sheet in 500 degree oven for 5 minutes. Makes 8 discs.*

Student Leaflet Answers
Picture This: (1) rock; (2) rainbow; (3) hand on Egypt; (4) empty tomb; (5) heart; (6) cup and bread; (7) U ; (8) bed; (9) calendar.

Meditation

As I meet you at the table of peace, O Lord God, nourish me with your yeasty bread of life. May your cup, filled with spiritual sustenance, flow from me and pour over the young lives of the children I meet this week.

Bible Scope

Luke 22:7-23; 19:28-48

Bible Text

Luke 22:7-23

Bible Story Focus

At their last meal together before his death, Jesus instructed his disciples how to remember him. This was the Passover meal.

Bible Memory Passage

Luke 12:22-31

Faith Nugget for Children

During meals with people we love, we can learn what it means that Jesus is our friend.

Anticipated Outcomes

The children will develop an appreciation for the celebration of the Last Supper and want to accept Christ as the center of their lives.

Essential Supplies

• Resource Box: Spiral Teaching Picture Book, Lenten Candle Cross Mat, cassette, Bible Verse Visual

• Student Leaflets
• Tape player
• String to tie around finger (6 in., 15 cm., per child)
• 20 to 25 items on the communion theme
• Four votive candleholders, four votive candles, matches
• Grape juice or drink in a glass or goblet, bread (unleavened, if available)
• Drawing paper, pencils, pens, markers, crayons, or colored pencils
• Pictures showing Passover meal or houses with upper rooms
• Soup crackers
• *If you use any of the Choices, collect the appropriate supplies.*

Early Preparation

1. On the table lay out twenty to twenty-five items that relate to the communion/remembering theme. Include flour, a bread pan, grapes, your church's communion plate, a glass, the Bible open to Luke 22, a pitcher, recipe cards, measuring spoons, napkins, and a note pad with the words *remember, remember* written on it. Arrange the items as a centerpiece on the work table.

2. Find the Lenten Candle Cross Mat in the Resource Box. Purchase four small glass candleholders and four votive candles to set on the mat. In your storytelling/worship center set the candleholders on the cross as shown. (For directions on how to make a wooden Lenten Candle Cross, see the back side of the mat.)

Place the bread and the glass with juice near the cross.

3. Put up the Spiral Teaching Picture in worship center.

4. Invite your pastor or other congregational leader to speak about communion. Make arrangements to use the area near your church's communion table. Ask the guest to show the trays used for serving the communion.

5. Memorize the Bible story so you can tell it fluently.

6. Learn the song "Let Us Break Bread Together" in the Student Leaflet. It is recorded on the Resource Box cassette.

7. Begin learning the Bible memory passage.

Lenten Candle Cross

Bible Background

The Feast of Unleavened Bread began at sundown and lasted for seven days. The feast coincided with the Passover that was one of the most important annual Jewish festivals. Every family sacrificed a lamb to recall the first such sacrifice when God rescued the Israelites from Egypt. As described in Exodus 12, God passed over the Israelite houses where lamb's blood had been sprinkled on the doorposts and spared the lives of their firstborn.

The Israelites prepared and ate unleavened bread, so-called because it was made without yeast or leavening. The bread also reminded the people of the hurried preparations their ancestors had made when Pharaoh finally allowed the Israelites to leave Egypt. Early celebrations of the Passover took place in homes, but by New Testament times pilgrims, like Jesus and the disciples, trekked to Jerusalem for the festival.

Jesus directed Peter and John to prepare the meal for the group. When they questioned him about location, it was clear that he had made prior arrangements. He instructed them to enter the city where they would meet a man carrying a jar of water. Finding this man would not be hard because carrying water was a woman's job. They followed the man into a house where the owner, upon hearing the prearranged words, showed them a large upstairs room, already furnished. Peter and John then bought, slaughtered, and roasted the Passover lamb and provided the unleavened bread, bitter herbs, and wine necessary for the special meal.

Bible Insights

At this meal Jesus instituted the Lord's Supper that Christians celebrate today. Jesus used the cup to symbolize the relationship between God and people. The bread represented the breaking of Jesus' body at his death. When Christians today celebrate this meal, we remember not only Jesus' death but also his invitation to follow him in daily living.

The Luke passage gives little directive for the inclusion of children in the communion service. How each congregation addresses this issue varies throughout the Anabaptist and Friends churches. If possible, let the children observe your congregation's communion service. Encourage them to wonder and ask questions. Use Responses #3 as a time to help the children process the meaning of communion in your tradition. Help the children experience Jesus' presence in their lives now as they look forward to church membership in the future.

BIBLE STUDY FOR TEACHER ENRICHMENT

TEACHING TIPS

Establish a mood with this lesson as soon as the children reach the classroom. Speak more slowly and quietly than usual. During the worship time help the children reflect on Jesus' life. Help prepare them for the time when each one of them will have the opportunity to dedicate his or her life to Christ.

Faith Nugget for Teachers

Through communion we learn about Jesus' life, we experience his presence in our lives, and we look forward to the completion of God's work.

● ● ▽ ●

STUDENT EXPERIENCE

Beginning Moments

1. As the children arrive, greet them at the door and tie a string around one finger of each child's hand. Or ask children to tie strings on each other's fingers, saying "remember, remember" as they tie the string. Be sure to tie a string around your finger too. Instruct the children to wear the strings until the end of class, adding the words "remember, remember."

2. Encourage the children to look for one to two minutes at the items on the worktable and name them. Take the children to the hallway and challenge them as a group to name all the items. When they struggle remembering so many items, point to the string on their fingers and say, "Remember, remember." Move quietly back into the room to the worship center for the Bible story.

Bible Story

1. Anticipate the Bible story. In the worship center ask the children to remember a special meal they have shared with family or friends. Have them close their eyes and remember the food, people, location, smells, sounds, flavors, and conversation. Invite the children to tell the class or one other person about this experience. After everyone has shared, point to the string on your finger and say, "Remember, remember."

Explain that Jesus also shared meals with his disciples. Our session will focus on one very special meal. This was his last meal with the disciples before he died. Many Christians call it the Last Supper, the Lord's Supper, or Holy Communion. It is a special event in the church all over the world, and we will learn how it started. Tell the class that Jesus knew how easy it is to forget, so at this meal he used two parts of the meal to help the disciples remember him.

2. Experience the Bible story. Create a quiet, reflective atmosphere by speaking softly and moving slowly. Ask a child to turn out the lights as you light the Remembering Candle. (Other candles are lit during Sessions 2, 3, and 4.) Speak in a reflective way, as if you were one of the disciples. Pause occasionally as if you are just recalling the way the events in the story happened. [*Stand by the worship center when you begin telling the story.*] Tell the story.

3. Wonder about the Bible story. Say the following in an unhurried, reflective way. Allow the children to wonder:
•I wonder how it felt to help Jesus prepare the meal.
•I wonder what the disciples would remember about Jesus after this special meal.
•I wonder how the disciples felt when Jesus said he would not drink again.
•I wonder how one disciple could betray Jesus. I wonder if I could betray Jesus.
•I wonder how it felt to be a special friend to Jesus. I wonder if I am just as special to him.
•I wonder what it means today when people celebrate the Last Supper.

After this time of wondering, discuss questions the children may have. Offer a prayer of remembrance: "Because we often forget things, dear Jesus, help us

each day to remember you. Amen."
Blow out the Remembering Candle.

Responses to the Bible Story

1. Draw pictures. Provide pencils, pens, markers, crayons, and colored pencils. Challenge the children to draw one part of this story. Show them pictures of houses with upper rooms and tables set up with the Passover meal prepared. Ask them to focus on the people and their expressions. Help them think what kinds of expressions—quiet, peaceful, surprised, worried, sad, happy—would be on the faces of the disciples and on Jesus. When children finish, help them put up the drawings in the room. Add a sign that says "Remembering Jesus."

2. Say the Bible memory passage with the children as they work on their drawings. Say one phrase or sentence and let the class repeat the words.

3. Prepare the children to listen to the pastor or church leader talk about communion. Together walk quietly to the communion table in the sanctuary. Listen to the guest explain how this meal is remembered in your church. Invite children to ask questions and make observations. Return to the classroom.

Closing Moments

1. Prepare for worship. When you reach the classroom door, explain that you want the children to sit in the worship center, to walk there quietly, and to think about remembering Jesus. Lead the children to the worship center.

2. Worship together. Relight the Remembering Candle. Turn out the lights and invite the children to focus on remembering Jesus, remembering his love for each one of them, remembering his death on the cross. Pass a tray of soup crackers and let each child

BIBLE STORY

The way I remember it—and that night was one I will never forget—there was the Feast of Unleavened Bread and the very same day was the Passover. Both of these were special Jewish celebrations that helped people remember the time when the people had to hurry and get out of Egypt. The angel of death passed over the houses where the blood of the lamb was smeared on the doorposts, and—what else?—the people had to prepare the bread so quickly that they didn't have time to wait for the bread to rise, so they made unleavened bread.

The way I remember it, all of us disciples had gone with Jesus to Jerusalem for these special festivals. I remember Jesus telling two of the disciples—was it Peter and John?—to go prepare the Passover meal for all of us. This was the first time we had been able to go to Jerusalem for this event. I remember Jesus telling these two disciples to go to the entrance of the city and to find a man carrying a jar of water. Then they were supposed to follow that man into a house and say to the owner of the house, "The teacher asks you, 'Where is the guest room where I may eat the Passover with my disciples?'"

Later on I heard that these two disciples had no problems finding the man or the house. That afternoon they went about preparing the Passover meal.

That evening Jesus took his place at the table. He sat in the host's seat [*Sit down*], and he said something about wanting to eat this meal with us before he suffered.

Then he did something I will never forget. He lifted up the cup [*Pick up the glass*], he offered a prayer, and said, "Take this and divide it among yourselves; for I tell you that from now on I will not drink of the fruit of the vine until the kingdom of God comes" [*Put down cup*].

I remember Jesus holding up a loaf of bread [*Pick up bread*]. He prayed again and tore it apart [*Tear bread*], gave each of us a piece, and said, "This is my body which is given for you. Do this to remember me" [*Put down bread*].

And then after he had eaten, he held up the cup again [*Hold up glass*] and said, "This cup that is poured out for you is the new covenant in my blood" [*Put down glass*].

Then I remember him looking around the table at each one of us and saying, "The one who betrays me is with me here, and his hand is on the table."

All of us disciples started talking, asking each other which one of us it could be that would betray our Master [*Pause*].

I remember all of this, and I am telling this to you so that you will remember Jesus too.

take one. Invite the children to close their eyes and, if they wish, to say a silent prayer that will ask Jesus to come into their lives. Pass out the Student Leaflets and sing "Let Us Break Bread Together." Or simply play the cassette while the children have their eyes closed.

3. Tell the children that you put strings on their fingers to help them to remember Jesus. Explain that you

CHOICES

Use these ideas in place of or to supplement the session plan.

will dismiss each child individually and that the lights will stay off. Excuse them with the words "Remember, (child's name) , remember." Be sure they take home their Student Leaflets.

1. For the Beginning Moments greet the children at the door with the instruction to "search around the church for a man carrying a jar of water. When you have found him, ask, 'Where is the guest room where we will eat the Passover with the disciples?' Follow the man's directions."

Write these instructions on a piece of paper that the children can carry with them. Follow the children as they search and guide them if they need help. When the children find this person, he directs them to a place suitable for the Bible story (back to the room if necessary), and he tells the story.

2. Play *Going to Jerusalem*. Ask the children to sit in a circle. The first person says, "I'm going to Jerusalem and I'm going to take _____." The child

names something that travelers to Jerusalem may have taken with them during Bible times. Appropriate responses would be "food," "sandals," "donkey," and "money."

Additional players repeat—in order—the previous responses and each adds his or her own word or phrase.

3. Sing "Let Us Break Bread Together." (See Student Leaflet and Resource Box cassette.) Explain the meaning of the words before singing each verse. Use guitar or autoharp accompaniment.

4. Make unleavened bread and eat it together for your closing worship. See the recipe for Golan Discs (unleavened bread) in the Teacher Preparation section, page 10.

5. Set up a book corner containing books on the Easter or remembering themes. Encourage the children to look at these books when they finish Responses #1.

Student Leaflet Answer
March through this maze.

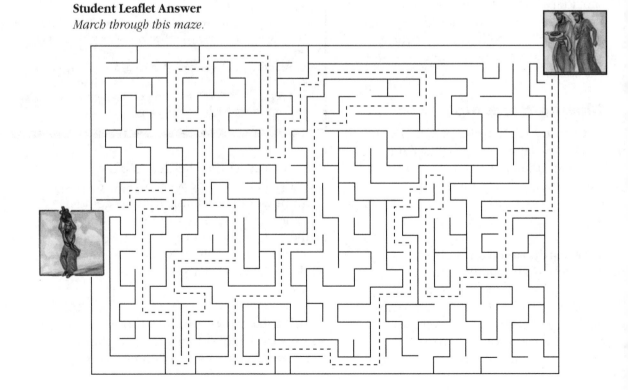

Use a remembering theme.

- Tie strings around fingers. Explain that people sometimes use things like this to help them remember. Ask for their suggestions of memory aids.
- Use ten to fifteen items for them to remember on the worktable.
- Play *Going to Jerusalem* (see Choices #2). Show pictures of Bible times to help them recall possible items to take on their imaginary trip.
- Tell the Bible story, including the triumphal entry in Luke 19:28-38. Wonder together.
- Offer options for the Responses.
1. Draw pictures on large sheets of construction paper.
2. Listen to the teacher read a book about Jerusalem or Easter.
3. Read "Kids in Jerusalem," a radio play in the Student Leaflet.
- Share in a time of worship and singing. Invite the children to let Jesus be a part of their lives.

3

TEACHING GRADE THREE

Use a Jerusalem theme.

- Search for a man with a jar of water (Choices #1). See Luke 22:10.
- Listen to the story. Have the man holding jar of water tell the Bible story from his point of view. Wonder together.
- Read "Jerusalem Today" in the Student Leaflet. Learn more about Jerusalem. Look at slides of the city or at pictures in books. Talk about its importance during Jesus' day. Ask someone who has visited or lived there to come to class.
- Work on a mural together. Allow a space of one to two square feet/meters of bulletin board paper per child. Offer ideas, but let children decide how the mural will depict the Bible story. (Ideas might include: tell the story from left to right in scenes depicting verses; draw only the Last Supper with disciples around table; draw a map of Jerusalem with scenes at the appropriate locations.) When children finish, they can complete activities in the Student Leaflet.
- Close with worship and singing "Let Us Break Bread Together."

4

TEACHING GRADE FOUR

Use a communion theme.

- Make "Jesus crackers." Show the children how to use a tube decorator to ice graham crackers. Write *Jesus* on the crackers.
- Tell stories of special meals the children have shared with family or friends. Tell your own story first.
- Read the story directly from the Bible.
- Listen to the pastor or church leader speak about communion. Allow time for the guest to talk about how communion is celebrated in your congregation. Prepare the guest for questions your children might ask.
- Worship. Pass out crackers decorated by the children. Children repeat phrases after you:

   [*Hold up cracker in both palms*]
   This reminds us of Christ's body
   [*Break in two pieces*]
   broken for you and me.
   [*Hold up crackers with both hands*]
   We do this
   [*Bow head*]
   to remember Jesus. Amen.
   [*Take bite of cracker*]

   As children eat crackers together, talk about the importance of fellowship in the communion experience. Talk about how remembering Jesus can help us in our daily lives.

5

TEACHING GRADE FIVE

Palm Sunday

2 The Suffering Servant

TEACHER PREPARATION

Meditation

Seize my spirit, Lord God of all, as I walk beside you on the road to the cross. Test my heart if I wander from the path. Judge my efforts as I clear the trail for others who want to follow you.

Bible Scope

Luke 22:22-53; 23:13-49

Bible Text

Luke 22:39-53; 23:13-49

Bible Story Focus

Jesus told his disciples that greatness was to be found in being a servant, not a king. His suffering and death showed the disciples what this way of life meant.

Bible Memory Passage

Luke 12:22-31

Faith Nugget for Children

Jesus died an unfair, horrible death on a cross. Jesus' death and his choice to die offer forgiveness and salvation to us.

Anticipated Outcomes

The children will understand that Jesus chose to die in order to share salvation with us.

Student Leaflet Answers
Who Am I? (1) Simon (of Cyrene); (2) Pilate; (3) soldiers; (4) Barabbas; (5) criminal; (6) Herod; (7) Jesus; (8) servant; (9) centurion; (10) Judas; (11) council; (12) angel; (13) disciples.

Word Find Key

Essential Supplies

•Resource Box: Spiral Teaching Picture Book, cassette, Lenten Candle Cross Mat, Jerusalem Map, Bible Verse Visual

•Student Leaflets
•Tape player
•Construction paper, scissors, glue
•Legos or other play building materials, poster board, folding table
•Two votive candles and holders, matches
•Bulletin board paper for mural, tempera, and paintbrushes or crayons
•Bible reference books that have pictures of typical buildings
•*If you use any of the Choices, collect the appropriate supplies.*

Early Preparation

1. **Put the Jerusalem Map** on the folding table with the Legos and Bible reference books.

2. **Place the Spiral Teaching Picture near the Lenten Candle Cross Mat** in the worship center.

3. **Put the supplies for making *Butterfly Feet* on the worktable.**

4. **Make cassette recordings of the Bible memory passage**—one for each child.

5. Practice telling the story.

6. Learn "Were You There?" (See Resource Box cassette.)

●●● ▽●

Bible Background

After Jesus' last meal with his disciples (Session 1) when his followers argued about who was greatest (Session 13), Jesus went with his disciples to the Mount of Olives to pray. This location, probably the private garden of a friend, had been Jesus' nightly retreat during the entire week (see Luke 21:37). Jesus prayed in agony (the Greek word is used for someone who is fighting a battle with fear).

Jesus was betrayed by Judas, arrested, tried, and sentenced to be crucified. A condemned criminal was forced to carry his own cross through the city streets to the crucifixion site by the longest possible route. In front of him a soldier carried a sign inscribed with his crime. Weakened by recent fasting, Jesus struggled until a soldier enlisted the aid of a bystander—Simon of Cyrene. (See Mark 15:21; Romans 16:13.)

Jesus hung on the cross under a darkened sky for several hours before crying, "Father, into your hands I commend my spirit." This was probably a childhood prayer he had been taught (without the word "Father") based on Psalm 31:5. Jesus took his last breath and died.

Bible Insights

Why did Jesus have to die? Children will struggle with this vivid account of Jesus' death. They will wonder about Judas, the traitor, who until that evening had been one of the disciples. Help them realize that it was difficult for all the disciples to understand Jesus' teachings when they were so different from the organized religion of the time. Even the faithful disciples showed how difficult it is to be faithful to God.

Faith Nugget for Teachers

The greatness of a servant calls us to share in Jesus' redemptive work.

BIBLE STUDY FOR TEACHER ENRICHMENT

TEACHING TIPS

When you offer choices during the response time, ask another adult to help you. Both of you can offer assistance and encouragement and help to keep the children focused on their activities.

A full-length mirror can help you practice the Bible story. When you tell a story, body posture, hand gestures, and facial expressions are very important. You will capture the children's attention if you have consciously thought about how you look when you are speaking.

STUDENT EXPERIENCE

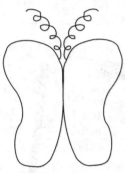

Butterfly

Lenten Candle Cross

Beginning Moments

1. Take off your shoes before you greet the children at the door. Ask them to remove their shoes (socks optional) for the session.

2. Direct the children to choose one of the following:

a. Make *Butterfly Feet*. The children take their shoes to the table, trace around shoe soles on construction paper, and cut out the sole patterns. Place <u>outside</u> edges of patterns together to form a paper butterfly, glue a center strip to hold pieces together, and decorate with curly paper antennae.

b. Build Jerusalem buildings out of Legos or building blocks. Use the Jerusalem Map and reference books on the worktable. Point out the city wall and other places mentioned in Luke 22 and 23.

Bible Story

1. Anticipate the Bible story. After about ten minutes of work, pick up your shoes (carrying them as if they were a platter of food for a king's table) and walk to each child. Ask him or her to quietly join the procession to the Bible story area. (The children should leave their shoes by the door for Closing Moments.) Walk slowly and sadly with your eyes focused ahead. When you reach the worship center, place your shoes near the Lenten Candle Cross Mat and sit down without saying anything. Light Remembering Candles #1 and #2 and wait for the children to be settled.

2. Experience the Bible story. Speak as if you were exhausted after a long walk. Tell the story.

3. Wonder about the Bible story. Pause for a few moments as you look at the Lenten Candle Cross Mat. Then offer these thoughts or allow children to question the events.

•I wonder how the disciples felt, when they finally realized that Jesus would be killed.

•How would you have felt if one of your very best friends was sentenced to die and you knew your friend was innocent?

Some of you may know that the story does not end there. We will finish the story next Sunday.

•Would any of you like to share how it feels when someone close to you dies?

•Which people do you like in the story? Which ones don't you like? How would you want to change the story?

Responses to the Bible Story

1. Encourage children to choose one of the following activities:

a. Paint a mural of the events. Have the children study the Bible story and paint a mural about it. They can organize the mural chronologically, or depict people, events, places, and their feelings in random order. Allow about 2 feet, 65 cm., of mural space per artist. Let older children work individually or in small groups to search the Scriptures for accurate details. Use this list of the major events:

1. The disciples argue about greatness at the Last Supper with Jesus (Luke 22:24-30).

2. Jesus and the disciples go to the Mount of Olives to pray (Luke 22:39-46).

3. Judas betrays Jesus before the arrest (Luke 22:47-53).

4. Peter denies knowing Jesus (Luke 22:54-62).

5. Jesus is beaten (Luke 22:63-65).

6. Jesus is brought before the religious leaders (Luke 22:66-71).

7. Jesus comes before Pilate (Luke 23:1-5).

8. Jesus comes before Herod (Luke 23:6-12).

9. Pilate sentences Jesus to death (Luke 23:13-25).

10. Simon of Cyrene carries Jesus' cross (Luke 23:26).

11. Jesus and two criminals are crucified (Luke 23:32-49).

b. Research information about Judas. Provide children's Bible commentaries and other reference material. The children can study the character of Judas, especially his reasons for betraying Jesus. They can give either an oral or written report.

c. Do *Who Am I?* in the Student Leaflet. The children can make up more riddles as time allows.

2. Memorize the Scripture. Say the passage together with the cassette recording you have prepared (Early Preparation #4). Give each child a cassette to take home. Suggest they play the cassette daily (e.g. before bed or during family devotions).

Closing Moments

1. Let the children share their Responses #1 with the group.

2. Gather at the worship center for worship.

a. Light two candles on the Lenten Candle Cross Mat.

b. Read Luke 23:44-49 (or ask a child to do this).

c. Sing a reflective song about Jesus that is familiar so you can sing without music. "Were You There" (Resource Box cassette), "Kum Ba Yah," or "Jesus, Remember Me," *Hymnal: A Worship Book* (Brethren Press, Faith & Life Press, Mennonite Publishing House, 1992) are good choices.

d. Say, "Jesus died for you and for me so that we may have the gift of life. This is a gift that we will share with God forever."

e. Extinguish the candles. Bow in silent prayer.

f. Ceremonially carry each child's shoes to him or her, or (for large classes) direct the children one by one to

BIBLE STORY

Walking. Walking. Walking. That's the way the disciples felt. For three years they had walked with Jesus throughout the countryside and into the cities. They had walked with Jesus to meet friends and to face the religious leaders. Now after the Lord's Supper when Jesus shared bread and wine with them and talked with them about being a servant, they were walking with him again. They were following him to the Mount of Olives where they would once again spend the night.

Walking. Walking. Walking. Arriving at the Mount of Olives, the tired disciples lay down to rest, but Jesus went on, about a stone's throw away. They knew he was praying, as he often did. Sleep was so comforting after the busy day [*Pause and close eyes for a moment*].

[*Open eyes wide, speak abruptly*] "Why are you sleeping?" Jesus was asking them as he walked toward them. He sounded very disappointed. "Can't you pray with me?"

Just then they heard noises and saw a crowd of people coming. Torches lighted their path. They were walking toward the Master as if they wanted to arrest him. Judas was leading them. As he leaned to kiss Jesus, the disciples realized that Jesus was actually being arrested. A scuffle started. One disciple drew his sword and cut off the ear of one of the servants in the crowd. Jesus said, "No more of this!" touched the servant's ear, and healed him.

Then they were walking and following Jesus as guards led him through the city to the high priest's house.

Walking. Walking. Walking. During the long night the disciples and his other friends had wondered what to do. Their Master had been treated as a common criminal. The men who were holding him had beaten him and made fun of him.

When day came, the disciples followed Jesus and the crowd—first to where the religious leaders were gathered together. There Jesus was accused of claiming to be the Son of God. The disciples began to worry because they knew that such a claim could get him killed.

They followed Jesus as he was brought to stand before Pilate, one of the government leaders. They followed Jesus as he was taken to stand before Herod, the man who ruled in Galilee where Jesus was from. Then he was taken back to Pilate. Walking with Jesus had never been so difficult.

They heard the order to crucify Jesus. Crucify Jesus? Hang him on a cross? Oh no!

Very hesitantly, they followed Jesus and the crowd out of the city and up the path that led to the hill shaped like a skull. There the disciples watched as his wrists and feet were nailed to a wooden cross, and he was left to die [*Extinguish candle #1*]. It was about noon, yet the whole land became dark until three o'clock in the afternoon.

Then Jesus said, "Father, into your hands I give up my spirit." He took his last breath and died [*Extinguish candle #2*].

The disciples and all of Jesus' friends would no longer be able to walk with him. They had followed Jesus for the last time.

carry shoes to a classmate. Say, "Walk in peace" as you say good-bye to each one at the door.

3. Be sure the children take home the Student Leaflets. Give the Jerusalem Moments Calendars to any

children who may have been absent
last week.

CHOICES

Use these ideas in place of or to supplement the session plan.

1. Set up a jigsaw puzzle appropriate to the season. Let children work on the puzzle as class begins. Talk with the children about how Christ's coming was expected for hundreds of years. Even after he arrived, it wasn't until his death and resurrection that people understood who he was. So it is with the puzzle. Not until it is finished can we see the complete picture.

2. Use the story figures to tell the story as you move them around the Jerusalem city that you built from Legos.

3. Tell the story as you process from place to place in the church or outside. Elaborate on the walking theme of the story or read the Scripture text from the Bible at each stop. Scenes

might include: Mount of Olives, Council Hall, Pilate's Palace, Herod's Court, Pilate's Palace, The Skull.

4. Visit a cemetery. Ask the caretaker to explain burial procedures. Follow this with a study of burial procedures in Jesus' day.

5. Build matchstick crosses using a cross made of heavy cardboard (see illustration) and <u>used</u> kitchen matches or new toothpicks. Allow 125 matches per cross. Spread a thick layer of white glue on the center area of cross. Lay four matches in an X shape. Continue spreading glue and alternating placement of matches to the end of each of the four extensions. Allow at least a day to dry.

Cross Pattern
Enlarge and use this pattern to create a cross from burned matches.

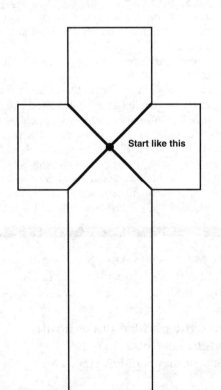

Start like this

3
TEACHING GRADE THREE

Focus on a walking theme.

•Make *Butterfly Feet*. Mount the finished butterflies on the ceiling and tell the children that following Jesus is like flying with butterflies. We can feel the freedom Jesus gives us.

•Build Jerusalem. Use the Jerusalem Map in the Resource Box to construct the city wall of Jerusalem out of Legos or small building blocks.

•Tell the Bible story. Use the Lego setting of Jerusalem and move the story figures around in it (or have children help move the people). Wonder about the story.

•Write thank-you notes to God. Let the children write prayers of gratitude for the gift of Jesus.

•Work on "Who Am I?" in the Student Leaflet. Children can make up "What Am I?" riddles. Example: I was the place where Jesus went to pray. Answer: Mount of Olives.

•Walk to the cross. During the last ten minutes, walk to a symbol of the cross in the sanctuary. Before walking, tell children to walk silently as they think about Jesus' disciples who followed him to the cross. Read a Bible verse and close with prayer.

4
TEACHING GRADE FOUR

Focus on Jesus as human.

•Walk on earth. Tell children to remove their shoes and socks. Have the children step into a basin of tempera paint and track steps on a wall-length piece of bulletin board paper. Explain to the children that Jesus too walked on earth. Even though we don't have record of his footprints, he was just as human as we are.

•Show pictures of present-day Jerusalem sites mentioned in the story.

•Tell the Bible story, pretending to be one of the characters in the story. Allow adequate time for discussion and wondering questions. This lesson may burden some children who may be hearing the story for the first time.

•Publish a class mini-newspaper. Write news stories (or draw pictures) that feature events from the Bible text. Provide a daily paper as an example for headlines and layout. Type the children's articles and mail the completed paper—named by the class—to each one during the week.

•Worship together around the Lenten Candle Cross Mat.

5
TEACHING GRADE FIVE

Focus on a death theme.

•Visit a cemetery. Make arrangements to take a field trip to a cemetery at the beginning of the session. Interview the church sexton or someone else familiar with present-day burial customs. Some congregations have their own burial plans. Check for alternative methods. (Or interview a funeral home director prior to class time, tape-record the conversation, and share this information with children.)

•Tell the Bible story in the cemetery.

•Worship together in prayer and song.

•Make crosses out of toothpicks or used kitchen matches and cardboard (Choices #5). Or make a wreath of crosses out of your choice of materials. As children work, read aloud about burial customs during Jesus' time.

•Write an obituary for Jesus. Provide daily newspapers for obituary samples.

Easter Sunday

The Walk to Emmaus

TEACHER PREPARATION

Student Leaflet Answers

See for Yourself: (1) d; (2) f; (3) a; (4) e; (5) b; (6). g; (7) c.

Meditation

Dear Jesus Christ, as I see you on the way to Sunday school, help me to recognize you as the Messiah. I invite you to my classroom so that you can reveal your true presence to the children I teach.

Bible Scope

Luke 24:1-35

Bible Text

Luke 24:13-35

Bible Story Focus

On Easter day two followers of Jesus on the road to Emmaus were amazed and filled with wonder when an unknown traveler (Jesus) joined them and explained everything to them.

Bible Memory Passage

Luke 12:22-31

Faith Nugget for Children

We are filled with wonder that Jesus is still alive and walks with us.

Anticipated Outcomes

The children will experience the surprise and joy of the resurrection.

Essential Supplies

• Resource Box: Spiral Teaching Picture Book, cassette, Lenten Candle Cross Mat, Bible Verse Visual

• Student Leaflets
• Seven story figures from the general classroom items
• A cloth for storytelling, several small boxes for houses, a small block for a table
• Tape player
• Easter stickers—one sheet per child and several extras
• Microscope(s) or magnifying glass(es) and small nature items
• Bible
• Three candles, matches
• Crepe paper
• *If you use any of the Choices, collect the appropriate supplies.*

Early Preparation

1. Move any large table(s) out of the classroom to allow room for drama and creative movement activities. Set up microscopes on a small table near a wall.

2. Prepare the worship center with the Lenten Candle Cross Mat, seasonal flowers, and the Spiral Teaching Picture.

3. Practice telling the story.

4. Copy Bible memory text from Resources, pages 94-95 (one set per child). Cut verses apart and clip sets of paper pieces together. Use reclosable plastic bags to keep these memory verses in class. Or make two sets for each child and send one set home.

5. Learn the circle dance to "Christ the Lord Is Risen Today" (Responses #1c).

Bible Background

Following the crucifixion, Joseph of Arimathea, a devout Pharisee and member of the Sanhedrin, received Pilate's permission to take Jesus' body down from the cross. The body was placed in a new tomb—unlike most tombs that contained bones of family ancestors. The customary embalming of the body did not occur because night was falling and the Passover began at dusk.

The women returned to the tomb, discovered the stone rolled away, and the body gone. Two angels told them that Jesus had risen; this news they reported to the eleven disciples.

Later that day while walking to Emmaus, about seven miles northwest of Jerusalem, two of Jesus' followers—Cleopas and an unnamed companion (possibly Cleopas's wife)—were joined by a stranger who professed ignorance of the recent events in Jerusalem. The stranger was Jesus. Although he was very near them, the two followers could not recognize him. They assumed he was another pilgrim returning home from the Passover celebration in Jerusalem, so they recounted the significant events of the past days. The stranger explained messianic Scriptures and, at the disciples' urgings, accepted an invitation to stay. When Jesus broke bread, the disciples recognized him,

and he disappeared from their sight. Immediately the two disciples rushed back to Jerusalem to tell their friends.

Bible Insights

Children like happy endings. After last week's tragic story, this account of Jesus' new life will satisfy that expectation. Children like surprises. That theme is repeated often. The women, disciples, and Cleopas and friend all were surprised by either Jesus' presence or absence.

The children need to wonder and ask questions. Through that wondering they will discover Jesus' part in their lives.

The Emmaus story contains the teaching that only through faith can one's beliefs in Jesus become real. When we invite Jesus into our homes and hearts, then we will begin walking with him forever.

Faith Nugget for Teachers

We are transformed at the miracle of Jesus' resurrection that brings new light to all of Scripture for us.

BIBLE STUDY FOR TEACHER ENRICHMENT

TEACHING TIPS

Give children space for the Responses by inviting another class to join yours. Then you will have two classrooms to use for drama and dance, and children will be able to work undisturbed by other groups. Arrange this with the teacher ahead of time.

STUDENT EXPERIENCE

Beginning Moments

1. Greet the children at the door with the words "The Lord is risen." Let the children choose an Easter sticker to wear.

2. Direct the children to the table where you have set up microscopes and magnifying glasses and tiny items from nature. Instruct them how to use the equipment and show them the Student Leaflet designs in tiny lettering: *Jesus Is Risen.* Let everyone have a turn with the microscope. Put the things away.

3. Lead the children quietly to the worship center for the story.

Bible Story

1. Anticipate the Bible story. Ask, "Why couldn't you read the words in the Student Leaflet?" When the children offer answers, explain that the disciples in our story saw Jesus, but their eyes could not recognize him. Talk briefly about times when identifying a person has been difficult.

Explain that our story about Jesus happens the same day as the women's discovery of the empty tomb. Read (or have a child read) Luke 24:1-12.

Tell the children that Jesus had more than the twelve (now eleven) disciples. He had other followers like the ones we will meet in today's story.

Lenten Candle Cross

2. Experience the Bible story. Light candles #1, #2, #3 on the Lenten Candle Cross Mat. Wait for the children to be quiet to begin telling the story. [*Put the boxes to represent Emmaus on one corner of the cloth; put the block table beside the town. Place two figures on the opposite end. Focus your attention on the figures and touch each as he speaks. Let your voice reflect the excitement of the disciples.*] Tell the story.

3. Wonder about the Bible story.

Look at the light of the candles for a few moments as the children absorb the story. Then offer statements similar to these:

•I wonder how the two followers felt when they recognized Jesus.
•I wonder how the two followers felt when they left Jerusalem.
•I wonder why Jesus didn't tell the people right away who he was.
•I wonder if I would have recognized Jesus if I had been one of the people who saw Jesus.

After a time of discussion, offer a prayer of thanksgiving and a time of silence when the children can think about inviting the risen Christ into their lives. Extinguish the candles.

Responses to the Bible Story

1. Offer several options for the children to choose:

a. Present role-play situations from the Bible story:
1. The meeting (vv. 13-16)
2. The conversation on the road (vv. 17-27)
3. The Emmaus meal (vv. 28-32)
4. The return to Jerusalem (vv. 33-35)

Each child takes the role of one character from the story. They can act out their parts, or you and the children can ask them questions in an interview setting.

b. Read the play "Seeing Is Believing" from the Student Leaflet.

c. Learn and present "Christ the Lord Is Risen Today" circle dance to music on the cassette. Dancers hold colored crepe paper streamers while moving in a circle as indicated.

Christ the Lord Is Risen Today
Circle Dance

Christ the Lord is risen today: [*Body moving to the left, left arm raised high, left palm leading; right arm slanted downward.*]

Alleluia: [*Arms and hands held high; body rotates around in a complete circle. Pivot in place.*]

All creation joins to say: [*Body moving to the right, right arm raised high, right palm leading; left arm slanted downward.*]

Alleluia: [*Arms and hands held high; body rotates around in a complete circle. Pivot in place.*]

Raise your joys and triumphs high: [*Starting low with hands at the sides, move to center of circle with hands going up.*]

Alleluia: [*Arms and hands held high; body rotates around in a complete circle. Pivot in place.*]

Sing, O heav'ns, and earth reply: [*Move back from center with hands going down*].

Alleluia: [*Arms high, body rotating around in place.*]

These movements may be repeated on all verses. Variation: on verses two and three, one child could do a solo on lines one and three with all children joining on lines three and four.

Reprinted from "Circle Dance" from *Worship through the Seasons* by Mary Isabelle Hock. Copyright 1987 by Resource Publications, Inc.; 160 E. Virginia St. #290; San Jose, CA 95112. Used by permission.

2. Continue learning the Bible memory passage. Make a copy of the Bible memory passage (Early Preparation #4) for each child. Cut the verses apart and challenge the children to put the Scripture passage back together. Let them use their Bibles for help. Collect the verses by sets and store for reuse.

Closing Moments

1. Let children present their Responses #1 for each other.

2. Hand out the sheets of religious Easter stickers and Student Leaflets as you dismiss the children. Challenge the children to spread the news about Jesus' resurrection as they stick stickers

BIBLE STORY

Cleopas and his friend were returning from Jerusalem where they had been for the Passover celebration. They were sad because their friend Jesus had died two days ago. They were sure they would never see him again. As they walked they talked about everything that had happened in Jerusalem the last few days.

[*Move the two figures along as you continue talking*] Cleopas said, "Can you believe that early, early this morning Mary Magdalene, Joanna, and the other women went to the tomb and found it empty? And two angels were guarding the tomb and told the women, 'He is not here; he has risen.' "

While they were talking about all of these things, suddenly someone came from behind and joined them as they were walking [*Place the Jesus figure between the two disciples; touch Jesus when he speaks*].

He asked the two, "What are you talking about?"

[*Touch Cleopas*] Cleopas said, "Are you the only stranger in Jerusalem who does not know the things that have taken place there in the past few days?"

[*Touch Jesus*] The stranger asked, "What things?"

[*Touch Cleopas*] Cleopas described how their friend Jesus died even though all of his followers were certain he was the one who would save Israel.

[*Touch the other disciple*] The other disciple explained how the women had gone to the tomb and couldn't find the body but had seen angels who said, "Jesus is alive."

[*Touch the Jesus figure*] The stranger said, "Oh, how foolish you are. You are so slow to believe what the prophets of old have written about. Wasn't it necessary that the Messiah should suffer these things and then enter into glory?"

Then the stranger began talking about the books of Moses and all the prophets as he explained how Christ's coming, death, and resurrection had been talked about for hundreds and hundreds of years.

The three arrived at Emmaus [*Move the three figures toward town*], and the stranger continued walking as if he were going on.

[*Touch Cleopas*] But Cleopas said, "Stay with us. It's almost evening." So the man came in to stay with them [*Move the figures around table*].

The stranger sat down to eat with them. Acting like the host, he took the bread, blessed and broke it, and gave it to the disciples.

Cleopas and his friend finally recognized the stranger. It was Jesus. Jesus had been with them all this time, and they hadn't known who he was.

As soon as they recognized him, he disappeared [*Remove Jesus quickly*]. Just like that [*Snap fingers*] he vanished from their sight.

[*Touch Cleopas figure*] Cleopas said, "It was really Jesus! How could we not have known it was Jesus when he explained the Scriptures to us?"

Immediately they got up and returned to Jerusalem [*Move the two quickly to the opposite end of cloth*]. They ran almost the whole way. There they found the eleven and all their friends [*Add the other figures*].

All the disciples were saying, "The Lord has risen indeed. He appeared to Simon Peter."

Cleopas and his friend told them about what had happened to them on the road, and how they had recognized Jesus when he broke the bread.

"We saw Jesus! We saw Jesus! The Lord is risen indeed!"

on their church friends. Tell them to use the greeting "The Lord is risen." Remind them to continue using their Jerusalem Moments Calendars for personal devotions during the week.

● ● ● ▽ ●

CHOICES

Use these ideas in place of or to supplement the session plan.

1. Play *Running Water, Still Water* during Beginning Moments. Blindfold one child. That child says, "Running water," and others move around the room until the child says, "Still water." The child searches with hands to find someone and tries to identify that person. If the child guesses correctly, the children change places. No talking (or giggling) is allowed. Relate this activity to the experiences of Jesus' followers when they discovered he was alive.

2. Write the story on stationery (or scroll) and pretend you have just received it from Cleopas (make changes necessary to indicate Cleopas is the writer). Then read it orally with expression.

3. Make crayon rubbings. To design Easter pictures, have the children lay letter stencils or flat objects from nature underneath construction paper and color the paper with flat side of crayon. Watch the pictures appear.

4. Talk about parts of nature that "die" in order for the species to live. Examples may include the pine tree (needs fire to germinate the cone's seeds), salmon and most spiders (lay eggs and then die), and annual flowers like marigolds and petunias (die when frozen and regenerate through dropped seeds). Make the distinction that unlike nature that continues its action of life-death-life, Jesus died and was resurrected only once. Through the cycles of nature, we are reminded of Christ's death and our new life.

5. If your class is small, choose one activity under Responses #1 and work on it together. Consider presenting it to another class. Plan for this activity ahead of time.

Shadow puppets

- Play *Running Water, Still Water* (Choices #1).
- Tell the Bible story using puppets. Wonder about the story and worship together.
- Color. Use crayons or pencil colors to complete the "See for Yourself" activity in the Student Leaflet.
- Or use creative dramatics. Retell the story in Luke 24:1-35. Assign parts to children: women, tomb, two angels, the eleven, Peter, Cleopas, friend, Emmaus, Jerusalem, Jesus, table. Read verse by verse and let the children act out what you have read. For dialogue let the children repeat parts of sentences after you. (Note: The children will speak expressively only if you do!)
- Do the circle dance, "Christ the Lord Is Risen Today" (Responses #1c).
- Pray together.

Leader: You are risen.
Group: You are risen.
Leader: Thank you, Lord.
Group: Thank you, Lord.
Leader: Amen.
Group: Amen.

- Discover a large Easter greeting. Tape large letter stencils on the back of a 3 x 5 ft., 1 x 1½ m., sheet of bulletin board paper. (Make extra letters out of cardboard, if needed.) The children rub paper with sides of crayons to discover the message: CHRIST LIVES!
- Tell the Bible story. Wonder about the story. Talk about the emotions of Jesus' followers—deep sadness, fright, excitement, doubt, and joy—all within the same day.
- Worship with the children.
- Write diary entries to answer this question: What would one of the disciples have written in his or her diary that first Easter night? Entries can be published in a church bulletin or newsletter.
- Retell the story using shadow puppets. Hang a white bedsheet and place a bright light bulb several feet behind the sheet. Attach dowel rods to poster board people and act out the story.
- Or learn the circle dance (Responses #1c).

- Use magnifying glasses or microscopes to see the tiny Easter greeting in Student Leaflet. Ask a science teacher for help if you do not know how to use a microscope.
- Have two young adults tell the story. Encourage them to use their own words to make the story meaningful. Wonder and worship together.
- Role-play. Let children volunteer to be Cleopas, Friend, Mary Magdalene, Joanna, Mary the mother of James, or Peter. Let the characters share their experiences or ask them questions.
- Melt crayons. Use potato peelers or dull paring knives to scrape pieces of crayons directly onto one 4 x 5 in., 10 x 12.5 cm., poster board. Put a second piece of poster paper on top, place between many layers of newspaper, and press with hot, dry (no steam) iron. Press ten to twenty seconds. Immediately after pressing, carefully pull papers apart. (They will be hot!) The results of this activity are worth the effort and will let children see the crayons in an unexpected, but recognizable, form. Cut around the edges for the desired shape. Mount art in a frame.

Jesus Appears and Departs

●●●

TEACHER PREPARATION

Student Leaflet Answers
Eyewitnesses: (1) Mary Magdalene; (2) Mary; (3) Cleopas; (4) Simon Peter; (5) the eleven and others; (6) Thomas; (7) Nathanael from Cana; (8) 500 people; (9) Saul (Paul); (10) apostles.

Meditation

With joy I reflect on your eternal presence, O Lord God. With joy I anticipate the time with the children. With joy I meditate as you reveal yourself to me.

Bible Scope

Luke 24:33-53

Bible Text

Luke 24:36-53

Bible Story Focus

After his resurrection Jesus came to the disciples to reassure them that he was alive and to explain to them that his life fulfilled the Scriptures.

Bible Memory Passage

Luke 12:22-31

Faith Nugget for Children

We are joyful because Jesus lives and fulfills all of the Bible.

Anticipated Outcomes

The children will feel the joy that comes with the knowledge that Jesus lives.

Essential Supplies

• Resource Box: Spiral Teaching Pictures, cassette, Lenten Candle Cross Mat, Bible Verse Visual

• Student Leaflets
• Tape player
• Four candles, matches
• Snack
• Bubble solution (Early Preparation #4), one- to two-gallon container
• Bubble wands (flyswatters, foil pie pans with centers cut out, large cookie cutters, etc.), towels
• Balloons—one per child
• *If you use any of the Choices, gather the appropriate supplies.*

Early Preparation

1. Prepare the worship center with the Lenten Candle Cross Mat, Spiral Teaching Picture, and flowers.

2. Learn the Bible story.

3. Prepare a snack.

4. Prepare the bubble solution: In a large container, mix ½ cup dishwashing liquid with 1 gallon of water. Add 2 tablespoons glycerine or corn syrup. Pour the solution into two or more containers. Double the amount for classes of more than ten. Check on an inside location for this activity in case the weather does not permit you to go outside.

5. Learn the songs "Asithi: Amen" (Resource Box cassette and Student Leaflet for Session 8) and "You Shall Go Out with Joy" (Student Leaflet, this session). (Both songs are recorded on the Resource Box cassette for Cycle A, Fall, Middler.)

BIBLE STUDY FOR TEACHER ENRICHMENT

Bible Background

This Scripture text directly follows the Emmaus narrative (Session 3) that took place the same day as the empty tomb's discovery. Our text relates another appearance of Jesus. Commentators generally agree that the story did not originate with Luke because of its striking similarity with John 20:19-23. It also has motifs similar to Matthew 28:16-20 and Mark 6:45-52. The story identifies the risen one as Jesus and emphasizes the physical state of his resurrected body.

In this text Jesus explained once again that his life, death, and resurrection all fulfilled Scripture (see Psalms 2, 16, 22, 69, and 110). One last time Jesus spoke of his role in fulfilling prophecy.

Bible Insights

Children can identify with the disciples who must have felt as if they had deserted Jesus just when he needed them most. They ask many questions just like the disciples did. They can understand how the disciples were frightened when they first saw Jesus. Help the children experience the joy that comes from knowing that Jesus lives and is an essential part of our faith. Encourage them to show that joy through praise.

Faith Nugget for Teachers

Jesus' resurrection amazes us and pushes us to reinterpret all of Scripture.

TEACHING TIPS

Discipline problems? Praise the children for every good behavior or idea. See how many times you can genuinely compliment the children. If problems do occur, send the offenders to the hallway with a card from your Consequence Box. (See Resources, page 90, for instructions on how to use a Consequence Box.)

STUDENT EXPERIENCE

Beginning Moments

1. As children arrive, greet them with the words "Peace be with you."

2. Direct the children to the table where you have laid out copies of the Student Leaflet opened to "The Great Catch." The children should fill in the blocks of this scavenger hunt-type game, answering the questions about themselves. Then they search for class members whose answers match theirs. The children sign each other's papers until all lines are filled. The children can work on the "Eyewitnesses" puzzle in the Student Leaflet until everyone is ready to move to the story area.

Bible Story

1. Anticipate the Bible story. Challenge the children to walk peacefully to the story area, sit down, and look at the Spiral Teaching Picture.

[*Light candle #1 on the Lenten Candle Cross Mat*] Say, "We light candle 1 to remember the last supper Jesus ate with the disciples.

[*Light candle #2*] We light candle 2 to remember Jesus' death on the cross.

[*Light candle #3*] We light candle 3 to remember that Jesus is alive and walks with us each day.

[*Light candle #4*] Today we light candle 4 to remember that Jesus lives with God, and we are filled with joy."

2. Experience the Bible story. Tell the story.

3. Wonder about the Bible story. Ask the children how they think the disciples must have felt. Offer these wondering statements:

•I wonder how I would have felt if I had seen Jesus with my own eyes.

•I wonder what I would think if I had heard Jesus explain all of this.

•I wonder if the disciples were sad to see Jesus go.

•I wonder how the Pharisees and other religious leaders felt when they heard that Jesus was seen again.

After the discussion time and while children are still sitting, lead into a time of worship.

Responses to the Bible Story

1. Worship together. Ask the children, "What were the disciples' first reactions after Jesus left them and went up into heaven?" After the children say, "They worshiped Jesus," tell them that we too will worship the Christ. Ask them to suggest ways of worship that are meaningful to them. If children have difficulty thinking of ideas, offer some of these: singing or listening to songs, prayer, reading Scripture, silent meditation, reading or listening to poetry. While maintaining a worshipful attitude, guide the children through the following activities. Allow for periods of silence.

a. Offer a prayer of thanksgiving and praise. Ask the children who wish to pray to say sentence prayers, thanking God for something special.

b. Listen to or sing "Asithi: Amen," Resource Box cassette.

c. Say the first two verses of the memory passage (Luke 12:22-23) in a quiet, reflective manner. Ask the children to repeat each phrase after you, pausing to think about the meaning.

d. Sing "You Shall Go Out with Joy" from the Student Leaflet.

e. Extinguish the candles and say, "Praise the Lord. Christ lives. Let us be joyful."

2. Have a time of fellowship and eat a simple snack together. As you talk with children, share examples of happy times you or they have experienced with other people.

Encourage the children to tell something new they discovered about each other when they did "The Great Catch" scavenger hunt in the Student Leaflet (Beginning Moments #2). Use this time to affirm our oneness in Christ and joy in his resurrection.

Closing Moments

1. Take the group outside for bubble making if weather allows. Encourage each child to dip bubble makers into a dishpan of solution. As the bubbles float away, help the children to realize that just as the bubbles disappear, so Jesus disappeared from sight when he ascended into heaven. The bubbles disappear, but the air trapped inside is still with us. When children finish, plan a time of hand washing with clean water.

2. Go back into the classroom. Be sure the children take home the Student Leaflets. Give a blown-up balloon to each child. Say a blessing, "Go in peace," to each child as he or she leaves.

BIBLE STORY

Here is where it happened—right here in this room in Jerusalem. I was one of the disciples—one of the men and the women—who had gathered together in this room in Jerusalem. The previous few days had been unbelievable. First, Jesus shared the Passover meal with us. The next day we watched as he died on a cross. Then two days later Mary Magdalene and others discovered the empty tomb and heard news from two angels that Jesus had risen.

That same evening here in this place, all of us disciples came together to eat a meal. First we heard news that Jesus had appeared to Simon Peter. Then two followers—one of them was Cleopas—arrived from Emmaus to tell us that they too had seen Jesus. We were amazed and excited.

This is the place. Right here. While we were talking, Jesus himself suddenly stood among us and said, "Peace be with you." Now that I think about it, his words should have made us feel good. Here he was, bringing peace to us. But we were surprised and frightened. A few of my friends told me later that they thought Jesus was a ghost.

Jesus stood right here. He said to us, "Why are you worried, and why do you doubt? Look at my hands and my feet. Touch me and see; a ghost does not have flesh and bones, as you see I have" [*Hold out hands*].

We were so shocked that we still couldn't believe this was Jesus. He asked for a piece of fish, ate part of it, and gave each of us a piece.

"While I was with you," he said, "I told you that everything that was written about me would happen. I came to fulfill the Scriptures."

Then we finally understood.

Jesus told us, "You are my witnesses of these things. Stay here in Jerusalem until you have received a special power from God. Then go out and preach in the name of Christ to all nations."

This is where it happened. Right here [*Pause*].

Then forty days after he rose from the dead, Jesus led us out of the city to an area near Bethany. We walked behind him like the Israelites followed Moses out of Egypt to the Promised Land. When we reached the place over there by Bethany, Jesus lifted up his hands [*Lift up both hands*] and blessed us. As he said the blessing, he left us and was taken up into heaven. I was there. I could show you where it happened.

For the first time, we fell to the ground to worship Jesus. Then we returned to Jerusalem with great joy and spent a lot of time in the temple praising God. I was there. I was there when Jesus, my Lord, ascended into heaven.

Amen. Amen. Amen.

CHOICES

Use these ideas in place of or to supplement the session plan.

1. Play *Sour Puss*. The children sit in a circle with "it" in the center. "It" goes to anyone in the circle, and asks a stupid question (e.g., Are cows purple? Are trees made of cement?). The one questioned must answer without smiling. If he or she does smile, the two exchange places. If the one questioned answers without smiling, "it" goes on to someone else. Follow this game with Choices #2.

2. Invite some joyful adults from your congregation to attend class during the session (no more than one per child). Ask them to be ready to share favorite Bible verses or praise songs. Incorporate their sharing into the Worship time. If your classroom is not large enough to accommodate all the people, make arrangements to use a larger room.

Use these two activities to show how the disciples changed from being sad to being glad. We can experience this joy because we know Jesus is alive.

3. Search your church's hymnbook for songs about joy. List these on the blackboard. Add other praise songs not in your hymnbook. Sing your favorites or learn a new one.

4. Celebrate at noon. Invite the children (and their parents) to a meal at the church or in a restaurant.

5. Make bubble prints as tray favors for hospital patients. Mix 2 to 3 tablespoons liquid tempera and $1/4$ cup bubble liquid (see recipe in Early Preparation #4) in an 8-ounce plastic margarine tub. The mixture should fill the tub only half full. Prepare two more tubs using other colors of tempera. Take turns. Each child blows through a straw until bubbles rise above the top of the tub. Then hold a 6 x 4 in., 15 x 10 cm., white construction paper (not glossy paper) over the bubbles until bubble prints appear. For additional colors, several prints can be put on the same paper. Dried prints can provide a background. Print Scripture verses, such as *"I am with you always." Matthew 28:20.* Use calligraphy pen or black permanent marker.

6. Give a new hymnal to each child in your class. Sing songs from these hymnals. ("Asithi: Amen" and "You Shall Go Out with Joy" are found in *Hymnal: A Worship Book.*)

Use a joy theme.

- Play *Sour Puss* during Beginning Moments.
- Tell the Bible story. Begin the story around the table in the classroom. At the point where Jesus led the disciples out of the city, lead the children out-of-doors. Conclude the story outside, emphasizing the joy the disciples felt as they remembered Christ's resurrection and ascension.
- Worship with bubbles. Stay outside to blow bubbles, using bottles of bubbles purchased in a store. As the bubbles burst, children repeat these lines: "You are the Christ. We share your joy. Amen."
- Wonder about the Bible story with creative imagining as children each "become" a disciple and describe their feelings.
- Search the hymnbook for songs of joy. Sing favorites, using percussion instruments as accompaniment.
- Watch popcorn pop. Eat the popped corn and talk about how Christ's presence in our lives makes us feel like bursting with joy.

3

TEACHING GRADE THREE

Use a shalom theme.

- Greet the children with the words "Peace be with you."
- Play *Run for Your Supper*. Form a circle. "It" walks around the outside of the circle and taps someone on the back. Then each child runs in opposite directions to reach the empty place. As the children meet each other going opposite directions, they must stop, shake hands, and say "Peace be with you" before running on.
- Tell the Bible story, emphasizing the peace that Jesus brought to the troubled hearts of the disciples.
- Discuss how Jesus brought and taught peace.
- Present "Appear and Ascend," a reader's theater Scripture reading in the Student Leaflet; OR
- Make peace posters. Look up the word *peace* in a thesaurus. Let the children work in groups to draw pictures of peace words, like *peace pipe, dove,* or *lay down one's arms.*
- Worship the God of peace and love. Sing "You Shall Go Out With Joy" (Student Leaflet) and repeat the Lord's Prayer.

4

TEACHING GRADE FOUR

Use a fish theme.

- Start with "The Great Catch" activity in the Student Leaflet.
- Tell the story from Peter's point of view and pass out fish crackers to involve children in the experience. Wonder about the story.
- Discuss beginnings of the early church (see Acts 1). Explain that the fish became a symbol of Christianity. During times of persecution, Christians used it as a secret symbol to discover if another person was a Christian. The letters of the Greek word for fish ("ichthus") are the same as the first letters of Jesus Christ, God's Son, Savior (in Greek, JCGSS).
- During worship time, offer the children the opportunity to follow Christ. Let a fishbowl (with fish) serve as the focal point. Invite children to see themselves as the fish swimming freely in the "Jesus" water. Outside the bowl, the fish would lie lifeless. Inside they are filled with the water of life.
- Make pins in the shape of fish.
- Have a picnic and go fishing together.

5

TEACHING GRADE FIVE

Pray This Way

TEACHER PREPARATION

Student Leaflet Answers
There's a Problem Here: Then <u>Jesus</u> said to his <u>disciples:</u> Therefore <u>I tell</u> you, do <u>not worry</u> about your <u>life</u>, what <u>you</u> will <u>eat</u>; or <u>about</u> your <u>body, what</u> you will <u>wear</u> (Luke <u>12</u>:22, NIV).

Resource Box Bible Verse Visuals
Use these Bible verses and symbols to help the children remember the story each session. Put them on your door, wall, or bulletin board and refer to them during the session.

Plan ahead for Session 6 Choices #4, page 44.
Ask several parents, other adults, or another group of children to come to your class wearing costumes and masks.

Meditation

I ask for your guidance, Master Teacher, as I teach.
I ask for your wisdom, Master Teacher, as I teach.
I ask for your patience, Master Teacher, as I teach.

Bible Scope

Luke 11:1-13

Bible Text

Luke 11:1-13

Bible Story Focus

Jesus taught his disciples a short and complete prayer. He encouraged them to ask boldly for what they need.

Bible Memory Passage

Luke 12:22-31 (22)

Faith Nugget for Children

When we ask for what we need, God will answer.

Anticipated Outcomes

The children will understand that God always responds to prayers, and they will seek to nurture their own prayer lives.

Essential Supplies

•Resource Box: Bible Memory Poster, Spiral Teaching Picture Book, cassette, Bible Verse Visual

•Story figures from the essential classroom items (enough for two families and one traveler. Add play animal figures as desired.)
•Student Leaflets
•Jerusalem Moments Calendars (Student Pack)
•Tape player
•Two small boxes (or the bottom 2-3 in., 5-7.5 cm., cut from a paper milk carton) to represent the two houses in the Bible story
•Hammers, nails, small wood pieces (Use a soft wood like pine.)
•Stationery or lined paper, envelopes, pencils or pens
•An empty chair
•Fishing equipment: dowel rods, string, snap-type clothespins, index cards
•Three beads to represent bread
•*If you use any of the Choices, gather the appropriate supplies.*

Early Preparation

1. For suggestions on room preparation for the quarter see the Writer's Page 9 in this Teacher's Guide. For bulletin board ideas see Resources, page 88.

2. Make door signs (Beginning Moments #1).

3. Ask an adult to help the children in the hall during Beginning Moments #1.

4. Prepare items for the story: two houses, seven or more characters, three beads for bread. Put up the Spiral Teaching Picture in the worship center.

5. Practice telling the story with the story figures.

6. Make one fishing rod for every three children. Tie one end of a 4 ft., 1½ m., string onto the end of a dowel rod. Tie the other end onto a clothespin.

7. Learn the song "Seek Ye First the Kingdom of God" (See Student Leaflet and Resource Box cassette.)

8. Put up the Bible Memory Poster from the Resource Box.

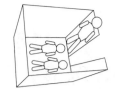

Milk carton house

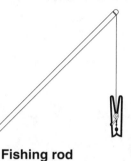

Fishing rod

• ▽ •

Bible Background

Although Matthew's Gospel also records the Lord's Prayer, only Luke recounts the parable of the friend at midnight. Though the modern-day reader might question the audacity of the late-night guest, traveling during the late evening hours was a common practice in Jesus' time. Most likely, a traveler would rest during the heat of the afternoon and journey late into the night.

Arriving late at someone's home could cause problems for the host. Food did not keep well, so those fixing it would prepare enough for only one day. When the food ran out, there was no more until the next morning. Hospitality was extremely important. Instead of insulting a guest, the host chose to awaken a neighbor and ask for bread. Borrowing from neighbors was a common practice. The amount borrowed would be returned when fresh bread was baked the next morning.

The bread requested was probably a loaf about the size of a stone that could be held in one's hand. Three loaves would be eaten by one person during a meal.

Houses in Israel were small, usually one room with a door. To keep out intruders, the head of the family would close the door and slide a wooden bar through rings on both the door and wall. The family slept close together on mats. Often animals were kept in the house

too. Disturbing the house's occupants meant bothering more than one person.

Bible Insights

This parable teaches persistence. From it we learn that God always responds to prayer. God is more willing to answer prayers than was the neighbor to answer the knock on the door.

Help the children establish regular prayer habits. Use your worship time each week to include the children's prayers, so they feel comfortable conversing with God. Stress that God will respond to our requests according to our needs.

Faith Nugget for Teachers

Persistence in praying is essential to effective faith development.

BIBLE STUDY FOR TEACHER ENRICHMENT

TEACHING TIPS

This lesson calls for at least one helper—one who can deal with pounding hammers, tangled fishing lines, and unusual prayer styles.

Not all children learn the same way. Kinesthetic learners need to touch objects of the lesson. They will express emotions with their whole bodies and will enjoy any activity involving the sense of touch. Instead of saying, "Keep your hands to yourself," you as the teacher should provide opportunities for active learning: field trips, games, plays, instruments, creative movement. If you meet the needs of the kinesthetic learners during Opening Moments, these children may be more responsive—and less disruptive—throughout the session. (See pp. 41 and 47 for ideas on teaching visual and auditory learners.)

STUDENT EXPERIENCE

Beginning Moments

1. As the children arrive, let them discover the classroom door closed. On the door is a sign that reads "Ask, and it will be given you; search, and you will find; _____ and the door will be opened for you." Near this sign put another one that reads "Look in Luke 11:9 to find the missing word. Do what the word says." Place a Bible near the door. Children will read the verse and discover that they are supposed to knock on the door. When you hear the first knock, open the door and joyfully welcome the children to the classroom. Have the first child welcome the next and so on.

2. Introduce yourself and be sure all the children know each other and feel welcome.

3. Invite the children to the area of the room (or outside) where you have arranged wood pieces, hammers, and nails. Caution the children to use the hammers with care. Tell them to try to pound the nail into the board using only <u>one</u> tap of the hammer. Then the children should put down their hammers and wait for instructions.

After each child has hammered once, explain that you want them to think of each time they pound as one prayer. Each nail represents a different prayer request. Sometimes when we pray, God does not seem to respond to our prayers. Sometimes we pray many times before we feel God has heard us.

Continue with the lesson and return to the hammers during Closing Moments, OR complete the hammer activity at the beginning of the lesson (Closing Moments #1).

Bible Story

1. Anticipate the Bible story. Quietly lead the children to the worship/story center for the Bible story.

Explain that in Israel the typical house had only one room that served as a living room, dining room, and bedroom. Cooking was done outside. During the day the door to the house was open, but at dusk the animals were brought inside and everyone in the family slept closely together. If there was any disturbance, all the people and animals were awakened.

Tell the children that when Jesus answered questions, he often told a story. These stories were called parables.

2. Experience the Bible story. [*From your Bible read Luke 11:1-4 to the children. Begin the story by putting story figures and houses in their places. People and animals are lying down. Traveler moves slowly to house A and waits at the door.*] Tell the story.

3. Wonder about the Bible story. Pause briefly after the story. Then offer these wondering thoughts:
•I wonder how I would feel if a neighbor and friend came for help in the night.
•I wonder what Jesus meant when he said, "Ask and it will be given you." Does God always give us what we ask for?
•I wonder how we can ask God for something we need.
•I wonder how we can know God hears us when we ask.

Allow the children to express their thoughts.

Responses to the Bible Story

1. Sing "Seek Ye First the Kingdom of God." Listen to verse 1 on the cassette; then sing it together. "Seek Ye First the Kingdom of God" is printed in the Student Leaflet.

2. Write letters to God. Direct the children to sit at the work table. Help the children understand that God is a friend, and that they can talk to God just like they talk to a friend. (Younger children may enjoy pretending that God is sitting in an empty chair in your room. Hand out stationery and pencils or pens. In friendly letter style, write several lines of a sample prayer on the board, using your own style of speech and not formal prayer language. Examples: "Hey, God, I want to talk with you about something. Jesus, you're a great friend because...." When the children are finished with their letters, they can address envelopes to God and post them on the bulletin board or place them in the offering plate.

When the children finish their letters, let them choose to read library books or use the hammers to pound small nails into the boards. Tell them they may pound one nail for each prayer request in their letter and add others for new concerns they think of.

3. Go fishing. Help the children learn that when they pray, their prayers may not be answered like they think they should be. Only God knows the best way to answer our prayers. Children should attach prayer requests to the ends of fishing rods, toss the lines into the water, and wait. When their prayers are answered, they receive either what they prayed for or something of equal blessing or better. Divide children into two unequal groups. To the larger group hand out dowel-rod poles equipped with lines and clothespin hooks. Each child writes a prayer request on an index card and tosses the line into the pond. A blanket or room divider separates the two groups of children. Children on the pond side read requests and gently tug on the line to return the cards with answers to the prayer requests. You can allow children to write the answers, or you can have some answers written ahead of class time.

Note that sometimes God uses other people to help answer our prayers. Have the children check answers with you before returning the lines.

BIBLE STORY

One time Jesus' disciples asked him how to pray. First he taught them the Lord's Prayer. Then he told them this story.

Late, late one night you hear knocking on your door [*Make knocking sound*]. You wake up and carefully step over your family members who are sleeping on the floor near you [*Move figure to door*], and you go to the door. "Who is there?" you ask in a sleepy voice. "It is I, (name), your friend from (*name a faraway familiar city*)" [*Point to traveler*].

This friend has come a long, long distance, and you know that you must let the friend in. You unlatch the door [*Figure pushes back door*], and your friend comes in [*Traveler moves into house*].

"Oh, I am so happy to see you. You must be very hungry after your long trip," you say. You remember that the last bit of bread was eaten at the evening meal, and you have no bread to serve this guest. If you tell this guest that you have no bread, the guest will feel bad. "Please relax and rest," you say [*Traveler lies down*]. You slip out the door and go to your neighbor's house [*Move out door and to house B*].

You knock on your neighbor's door [*Make knocking sound*] even though you know it is midnight. [*Loud whisper*] "Friend," you say, "please lend me three loaves of bread for a friend of mine has come a long way. I have nothing to feed this dear friend."

But your neighbor [*Neighbor figure turns over in bed*] answers from inside [*Muffled voice*], "Don't bother me; the door has already been locked, and my children are with me in bed. I can't get up and give you anything."

You keep knocking [*Make knocking sound*] and asking, "Please, neighbor, help me out," knocking [*Make knocking sound*] and asking, "Please, lend me some bread," and <u>finally</u> the neighbor brings you three loaves of bread [*Neighbor gets up, moves to three loaves, carries them to door, opens door, and gives loaves to you*].

This neighbor doesn't do this because of your friendship, but because you were persistent, and you kept asking [*Neighbor goes back to bed; you carry loaves to traveler in house A*].

After Jesus told this story, he said to the disciples, "Ask and it will be given you; search and you will find; knock and the door will be opened for you."

For everyone who asks [*Stretch out open hand*], receives [*Use free hand to "put" something in open hand*], and everyone who searches [*Hand over eyes*], finds [*Point to something in the distance*]; and for everyone who knocks [*Knock with the knuckles of one hand on the palm of your other hand*], the door will be opened [*Move arm as if door*].

4. Draw attention to the Bible Memory Poster. Explain that you will work together to learn this entire passage during the quarter. Repeat verse 22 together. Say it several times, varying the tone and intensity of your voice so the children imitate you.

Closing Moments

1. Return to the hammers. Talk briefly about the meaning of each pound on the nail (one prayer) and each nail (one prayer request). Suggest that they stop after each pound and listen to what God might be saying to them. Invite the children to pound the nails completely into the boards. The children can help each other. Ask what they have learned. (We should never give up praying. God may respond to our prayers in surprising ways. We should listen to God speaking to us. We should remember that God cares for all people, and we can pray for other people too.)

2. Invite the children to think about something or someone they want to pray about. Invite them to share their requests. As the children bow their heads, ask them to close their eyes. Suggest that they picture their requests being answered by God. Ask for a time of silence. Then say the Lord's Prayer. (Children who know it may say it with you.)

3. Show the children the Jerusalem Moments Calendar from the Student Pack. Explain how they can use it everyday throughout the quarter for their personal devotions.

4. Excuse the children one by one with a hug or smile. Be sure they take home the student leaflets and the devotional calendars.

● ● ● ▽ ●

CHOICES

Use these ideas in place of or to supplement the session plan.

1. During Beginning Moments use an old telephone to "talk" with God. During Closing Moments the children can share their prayer requests by talking on the telephone.

2. Use the sound-effects story, "A Friend at Midnight," in the Student Leaflet to retell the Bible story. Children can volunteer for parts to perform alone or in small groups, or all children can do all parts.

3. Bring an old door to class or make a door out of paper. It can symbolize prayer. Pound nails into it during Opening Moments, tack letters to it, or use it for graffiti prayers. Let the children write short prayers on it with wide-tip markers. Another option is to write on the door a list of prayer requests that the children suggest. During the quarter the children can write beside the requests when and how the request was answered. Other requests can be added.

4. For large classes set up three learning centers. Let the children choose an activity.

a. The Asking Center has supplies for making prayer chains. On 1 x 4 in., 2.5 x 10 cm., strips of construction paper, the children write the names of people. Strips are glued or stapled together to form chains. At home the children can use the chains to pray for these people during personal prayer time.

b. In the Searching Center children highlight prayer requests in church bulletins, newsletters, or magazines, or they can complete the "Pray, Pray, Pray" puzzle in the Student Leaflet.

c. In the Knocking Center children can mime the action of the Bible story.

• Hammer prayer requests. Use only one hammer for Beginning Moments #3. Let the children take turns pounding one prayer request to God. Complete the hammering activity at the beginning of the session.

• Tell the story with the story figures.

• Let children respond. The children can choose one of these activities:

a. Read the sound-effects story, "A Friend at Midnight," from the Student Leaflet. For variety, assign one part to each child, several parts to each child, or all parts to everyone. Offer the reading job to a good reader. Stress cooperation rather than competition.

b. Make prayer chains. Send the paper pieces home with the children to complete with family members. Encourage the children to use these as part of personal or family devotions.

c. Write letters to God. Before posting any of these for others to read, ask the permission of each writer.

• Worship together. Share prayer requests and sing "Seek Ye First the Kingdom of God."

• Hammer prayer requests (Beginning Moments #3). Supply one hammer for every two or three children and let them work together on pounding prayer requests.

• Tell the Bible story using puppets. Set up two cardboard boxes to represent the houses, and use two puppets to represent the homeowner and the traveler. Allow time for wondering and questions.

• Fly airplane prayers. Children can write prayer requests on standard-size typing paper, fold the paper into airplanes, and fly them to each other. They write answers to the prayers on the same paper and return the planes via air.

• Do "Pray, Pray, Pray" and "There's a Problem Here" in the Student Leaflet.

• Return to the hammers. Pound the nails completely into the boards. Relate this activity to our prayer lives (Closing Moments #1).

• Worship together. The children can share prayer requests and bow in silence as they picture the requests being answered by God.

• Count the doors in your church or in your area of the building. Show the children the door to your classroom and compare doors to prayers and talking with God.

• Illustrate the Bible story. While you tell the story, draw pictures on a paper taped to the back of the classroom door.

• Discuss questions about unanswered prayers and methods of praying. Review the meaning of the Lord's Prayer. Ask your pastor if you are uncomfortable discussing these questions.

• Have the children mime the Bible story. Exaggerate the actions so the story's meaning comes through without words. Children may want to present this story to the congregation during worship time; OR

• Encourage the children to rewrite the Lord's Prayer using "kid's language" (the common style of speech that children use).

• Worship together. Share a time of prayer as you help children focus on God. Kneel together in adoration of God.

Clean Up the Inside

TEACHER PREPARATION

Student Leaflet Answers

Pitcher Puzzle:
(1) Blessed are the pure in heart, for they will see God; (2) Love the Lord your God with all your heart; (3) Create in me a pure heart, O God; (4) The Lord looks at the heart.

Bible Memory Rebus: For life is more than food and the body more than clothing (Luke 12:23, NRSV).

Window Cleaner Recipe

A simple, safe window-cleaning recipe is ¹/₂ cup lemon juice or white vinegar mixed with 1 gallon warm water. If your class's eagerness sometimes causes accidents to happen, use this recipe, and you won't have to worry about harmful chemicals while the children spray the windows. This solution is also more environmentally friendly.

Meditation

Fill me, O Lord, with your purity, righteousness, and wholeness. Tip the pitcher of my soul, and make me a never-ending vessel of your love as I pour myself into the hearts and minds of these children.

Bible Scope

Luke 11:34-44; Galatians 5:19-21

Bible Text

Luke 11:37-44

Bible Story Focus

Jesus taught that we must take care of what is inside of us and not pay attention just to the outside.

Bible Memory Passage

Luke 12:22-31 (23)

Faith Nugget for Children

Jesus taught us to take special care of what is on the inside of us.

Anticipated Outcomes

The children will accept their own outward appearances, learn about the Pharisees, and recognize the importance of caring for their inner selves.

Essential Supplies

•Resource Box: Spiral Teaching Picture Book, cassette, Bible Memory Poster, Song Chart, Bible Verse Visual

•Student Leaflets
•Tape player
•Bath towel
•Pieces of bulletin board paper or newsprint big enough to draw around each child
•Markers, large sheets of paper for tracing silhouette (one per child), lamps, extension cords, pencils
•Scissors
•Basin of water, dishwashing liquid, dishcloth, dish towel, dirty cup
•Magazine pictures of people
•Window cleaner, rags
•*If you use any of the Choices, gather the appropriate supplies.*

Early Preparation

1. Set up an area for life-size drawings. Test light and sitting positions for silhouettes.

2. Stain inside of a cup using strong coffee solution (¹/₄ cup instant coffee, 1 cup water). Allow it to sit overnight to set the stain. Fill a basin with water and soap.

3. Set up the Spiral Teaching Picture for Session 6. On a notecard write the word *Pharisee* in large, dark letters and place the card beside the picture.

4. Learn the song "Wash Me." Use the Resource Box cassette and Song Chart to help you. The song also is printed in the Student Leaflet.

5. Tell the Bible story from the point of view of the Pharisee. Invite a high school youth or someone interested in drama to present the story. Ask the individual to dress in costume if possible. The storyteller should use a tone of voice to indicate that he had caught someone doing something wrong, and then he himself was accused of a worse fault.

6. Ask church janitor for permission to clean windows or glass doors.

If you plan to do Choices #5, plan ahead. Notify the children to bring three to five magazines from home, so they have magazines with pictures of their favorite things. Ask for magazines that can be cut up.

Bible Background

The Pharisees were a group within the Jewish faith who came into prominence during the second century B.C. They were anxious to spread the Jewish way of life as a definite and strict discipline for all of human activity. One meaning for Pharisee is "separated people." While trying to interpret the Law and its effect on the trivial aspects of life, the Pharisees often were harsh and insensitive. Jesus knew that many of their rules were just human ideas about God's laws. Jesus criticized this legalism.

For example: The Pharisee who invited Jesus for a meal was shocked when Jesus did not wash his hands before eating. This washing was a kind of ceremonial cleansing. The law required that a tiny amount of water (only enough to fill one and a half eggshells) be poured over the hands before eating and between courses.

Jesus used everyday objects to make his point. The cup was either a cup or goblet; the dish was really a platter. The meal itself was probably a breakfast meal after the morning temple prayers that most Pharisees attended.

Some of the Pharisees did not like Jesus. When they saw that Jesus' followers picked grain to eat on the Sabbath (Matthew 12:1ff.) and that Jesus cured people on the Sabbath, they confronted him. Jesus recognized that the Pharisees' understanding of the Law varied greatly from the original intent laid down by God. Jesus tried to set things straight. This angered the Pharisees who sought ways to get rid of Jesus.

Bible Insights

Help children understand that it is sometimes hard for people to interpret what God's laws mean. Sometimes we think we are following the Bible's teachings but we misinterpret them and end up with wrong attitudes and actions. How we act should be the same as how we believe. By washing only the outside of our bodies, we are left with unclean hearts. We should never imitate the Pharisees and think we are better than other people.

Faith Nugget for Teachers

The light and cleanness we have on the inside will affect how we act and live.

BIBLE STUDY FOR TEACHER ENRICHMENT

STUDENT EXPERIENCE

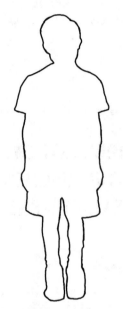

Body silhouette

Head and shoulder silhouette

Beginning Moments

1. Greet the children at the door as they arrive. Use a clean towel and pretend to wipe off each person before allowing him or her into the room. Say, "I need to make certain you are clean before you can come into the room." Wipe yourself and any other adults in the room. After this pretend wiping, comment about how clean each person looks.

2. Trace around each child's body. Direct the children to the area set up with materials for tracing. This activity will help each child focus on and accept his or her outward appearance. Select one of these options:

a. Using large rolls of newsprint or bulletin board paper, trace around each child's body. The children lie on the paper on the floor. Let children choose partners if they wish. The partners can draw around each other. Each child cuts out his or her own image and colors hair, eyes, and clothing with markers or crayons.

b. Trace only the silhouettes of heads and shoulders. The child sits in a chair with one shoulder touching the wall. A desk lamp is used to form a silhouette on paper attached to wall. Work quickly so the children do not have to sit still very long. Or set up several stations and ask another adult to help you.

Mount these life-size drawings or silhouettes on the classroom or hallway walls with a sign "Who Am I?" Leave these up all quarter so visitors can identify the children.

While you and the children trace around bodies or heads, offer the Bible Memory Rebus puzzle in the Student Leaflet to the children who are not involved in the project. To work the rebus, the children should concentrate on the sounds of the words and letters. For example, the EYE in the second word is the middle sound in the word LIFE.

Bible Story

1. Anticipate the Bible story. At the worktable use a basin of soapy water and a dirty cup to illustrate verse 39. As you wash only the outside of the cup, explain that you want to make sure you get the cup really clean. Children will quickly catch on that the inside is still dirty. Explain that once when Jesus ate a meal at the home of one of the religious leaders—a Pharisee—Jesus compared somebody to a cup. Challenge the children to listen closely to the story. Ask the children to follow you quietly to the worship center for the story.

Refer to the word *Pharisee* on the note card beside the teaching picture. Give the following definition: a member of a certain group of Jews who believed in strict obedience to the religious laws. Tell the story.

2. Experience the Bible story. [*The storyteller enters classroom without knocking, obviously upset about what Jesus told him. He paces floor, wrings hands, and uses other mannerisms to indicate he is upset.*]

3. Wonder about the Bible story. Pause for a few moments as the children absorb what they have heard. Then offer wondering comments like these:

•I wonder about this Pharisee.
•I wonder how the Pharisee may have changed after this meal with Jesus.
•I wonder if I might be like the Pharisee.
•I wonder what Jesus sees on the inside of me.
•What things make me dirty on the inside? I wonder how I can keep clean on the inside too.

Invite children's comments or questions.

Responses to the Bible Story

1. Teach the children the song "Wash Me." Sing or listen to the cassette while the children follow the words on Resource Box Song Chart. Explain that this simple song asks God to make us clean, to wash away all the things that keep us from thinking about God. It is a prayer to be sung joyfully with hands and eyes lifted up in prayer.

2. Discuss magazine photos of a variety of people. Ask the children to make assumptions based on what they see in each picture. For example, show a photo of someone begging for food, and ask, "What do you think this person is like?" When the children respond with "poor," "hungry," "from a poor country," "from a big family," initiate a discussion about assumptions. Help the children understand that outward appearance does not tell what one is like on the inside.

3. Hand out window-cleaning spray bottles and rags or newspapers. (Caution children NOT to point the bottles of spray cleaner at each other or themselves.) Clean the windows in the classroom or down the hall. Tell the children to remember that cleaning who we are is like washing the windows. Both the inside and outside should be clean. Compare God to a great big window cleaner who is willing to clean up our hearts if we just ask for a big spray of cleansing. Use this time to visit with the children as you work with them. Collect cleaning supplies.

Closing Moments

1. When you have finished with the window cleaning, return to the classroom. Gather the children in a tight circle and say a prayer, asking God to fill the lives of each one with loving thoughts and actions. Sing "Wash Me." Invite the children to use the same motions they used when wiping the windows to add rhythmic movement to

BIBLE STORY

That Jesus! I invited him to eat a meal in my home. I wanted to learn to know this man that everyone in the community was talking about. I thought because I was a Pharisee, I should know what this man was thinking. I thought we would have a nice, quiet meal. I figured that because he was from a Jewish family in Galilee, he would at least follow the Jewish laws about eating.

Was I ever wrong! Wrong, wrong, wrong. Jesus said, "Sure, I'll be glad to come." He came inside and sat down at my table. My servants brought in the wonderful food and set it in front of him. Jesus just started eating! He didn't wash his hands and didn't even *dip* his hands in water like our law commands.

Why, when this happened, I was surprised—shocked would be a better word.

Jesus saw my discomfort and said, "Now you Pharisees, you clean the outside of the cup and the outside of the dish but inside you are greedy and bad.

Who was this man, I wondered. He insulted me in my own house!

Jesus continued, "You are foolish! [*Holding up cup*]. Did not the one who made the outside also make the inside?"

He called me foolish. He told me I was greedy and bad even though I was just trying to follow the rules. We Pharisees like to follow the rules of the Jewish faith. We believe that there are very strict rules for every part of life. We follow those rules closely.

That Jesus! Then he told me, "So give your inner self as an offering to God, and then everything will be clean for you."

Who is this Jesus? What does he mean? That is a strange riddle! [*Storyteller exits*].

the song. Sing the song several times as you lead a musical procession around the room or down the hall.

2. Dismiss the children with the joyful benediction "Jesus can make you clean on the inside. Go in peace." Be sure they take home the Student Leaflets. Give Jerusalem Moments Calendars to any children who did not receive them last week.

Plan ahead. *Tell the children you may go for a walk next week and that they should dress appropriately.*

CHOICES

Use these ideas in place of or to supplement the session plan.

1. Wash hands. As the children arrive, wash their hands with soap and water (Beginning Moments #1).

2. Take photographs of the children—individuals or groups. Use these pictures to decorate a bulletin board or classroom door. This activity will take less time than the options in Beginning Moments #2.

3. Read the Bible story as if it were a letter sent to you by a Pharisee friend.

4. Ask several parents, other adults, or another group of children to come to class wearing costumes and masks. Welcome your costumed guests to the classroom. Give children clues to identify the individuals. The clues reveal only positive inner attributes and not external ones. For example, do not use hair color to identify the person. Rather, talk about his willingness to help new people in his neighborhood.

5. Decorate ME boxes. Explain to the children that sometimes we are very different on the outside and inside. Challenge them to decorate the outside of a shoebox to show what they are like on the outside and to show on the inside of the shoebox what they are like on the inside. The children cut out magazine photos and glue pictures onto the box. Instruct the children to completely cover the box (and lid) with pictures. Provide a sample you have made that shows how you are different on the outside and inside.

6. Have the children each wash a dirty cup during Closing Moments if you do not wash windows. As they wash the cup, help them see God cleaning their lives—both inside and out. Sing "Wash Me." Serve ice water or lemonade in the clean cups.

7. Play the *ACTS* game (Resource Box). (See Resources, page 92, for directions.)

•Trace around bodies (Beginning Moments #2a). Direct the children to add only one or two details with a marker (like brown hair and red shoes) so that others will have to work hard to guess who they are.
•Talk about being dirty. Let the children share stories about times when they felt very dirty on the outside.
•Wash the outside of a dirty cup. Exaggerate the washing and talk about how pleased you are that you are cleaning the cup so well.
•Read the Bible story in letter form. Ask a church member to dress as a postal carrier to deliver the letter to you. Share a time of wonder.
•Sing songs, hymns, and choruses about water, washing, and cleaning. Teach the class "Wash Me."
•Identify disguised guests (Choices #4). Invite a parent or older church friend for each child. Provide masks for these special helpers or let them wear their own disguises.
•Wash cups. Let each child wash a dirty cup. Serve a drink in the clean cups.
•Worship with your guests.

3

TEACHING GRADE THREE

•Wash hands. As the children arrive, wash their hands with soap in a basin of water. Rinse in clean water and towel dry.
•Trace silhouettes. Mount these on the classroom wall. Alternate sitting positions so that when mounted, the silhouettes can "face" each other.
•Listen to a storyteller. Let the guest, dressed as Pharisee (or Pharisee's wife), interrupt your work on silhouettes.
•Wonder about the Bible story. Reread the Scripture from Luke 11:34-41 and let the children ask questions.
•For Choices #4 invite another class to participate. Bring masks and have children put them on behind a curtain. Wearing a mask, each child in turn reveals only the head with mask, and members of the other class try to guess identities by clues the teacher gives.
•Wash windows. Pair children in twos to wash windows. Stress cooperation rather than competition.

4

TEACHING GRADE FOUR

•Photograph class members in a group. Ask a parent or church photographer to take the photograph so you can join the class members. Send a copy of the photo to each child with an Easter card.
•Wash a dirty cup. Let a child help. Contact the person earlier in the week so he or she knows to wash only the outside of cup. Pretend to choose the person at random.
•Listen to the storyteller. Let the children ask questions of the storyteller before he or she leaves.
•Discuss Pharisees. Provide Bible dictionaries or commentaries and have the children look up information about Pharisees.
•Play the *ACTS* game in Resource Box (Choices #7). For large classes divide into small groups or offer an alternate activity like the ME boxes (Choices #5).
•Together with the children, wash cups, pitcher, and utensils for making punch.
•Worship God with clean cups offered to symbolize clean lives.
•Prepare punch and serve drink.

5

TEACHING GRADE FIVE

Don't Worry, Trust God

TEACHER PREPARATION

Plan ahead for next week. Collect supplies for making wire sculptures. See Essential Supplies, page 52.

Add a floral touch. An avid gardener may be willing to share anemones with your class. A variety of fall-planted bulb anemones bloom in early spring; anemones from seed are planted in spring and bloom in summer.

Student Leaflet Anwers
Plants in the Bible: PALM, OLIVE, CEDAR, ONIONS OR MELONS, COTTON, FRANKINCENSE, FIG, CINNAMON, WHEAT, MYRRH, HERBS, EBONY, GARLIC, BARLEY, LILY, SYCAMORE.

Meditation

As a sunflower stretches to face the sun, may I always turn my face toward you, O loving God. As I focus on your presence, may the worries in my life float away with the wind.

Bible Scope

Luke 12:22-32

Bible Text

Luke 12:22-32

Bible Story Focus

God loves and cares for all of creation, so we don't need to worry.

Bible Memory Passage

Luke 12:22-31 (24)

Faith Nugget for Children

We trust God because we know God cares for us.

Anticipated Outcomes

The children will understand the Bible's teachings about worry, discuss worries and ways to conquer them, and feel God's care.

Essential Supplies

•Resource Box: Spiral Teaching Picture Book, cassette, Bible Memory Poster, Song Chart, Bible Verse Visual

•Student Leaflets
•Tape player
•Magazine pictures of plants and animals, paper, pencils
•Chalkboard or dry erase board and chalk or dry erase markers
•Blankets
•Bible
•Flowers
•Drawing paper, crayons
•*If you use any of the Choices, gather the appropriate supplies.*

Early Preparation

1. Ask a trained counselor to talk with the children about worries and fears.

2. Remind the children of a possible walk outside, and ask them to wear or bring appropriate shoes and clothes.

3. Learn the song "Do Not Worry" (Resource Box cassette and song chart) so you can teach it to the children. The song also is printed in the Student Leaflet.

4. Set up a display featuring magazine pictures of birds, animals, flowers, plants.

5. Memorize Luke 12:22-31 (NIV or NRSV).

6. Prepare or purchase one small flower for each child.

7. Set up the Spiral Teaching Picture in the worship center.

Bible Background

Crown anemones (*Anemone coronaria*) are traditionally considered to be the flowers Jesus referred to as the "lilies of the field." Because true lilies do not grow in the fields, the term simply means "pretty wild flowers." Usually scarlet (but sometimes purple, pink, blue, and white), the crown anemone is a favorite flower of spring when it colors the Mediterranean hills.

The wealthy King Solomon could not clothe himself in beauty equal to that of the flowers in the field. Only God can create real beauty.

The raven is a member of the crow family. In Palestine specific birds include the rook, jackdaw, jay, fan-tailed raven, hooded crow, and raven. Ravens build huge nests of sticks and twigs on crags and trees, lining them with bits of cloth and paper. The raven (*corvus corax*) is the largest (25 in., about 60 cm.), long and black all over.

Easily recognized because of its size and wedge-shaped tail when flying, the raven serves as a scavenger, eating not only dead or weak animals but also fruit, especially dates. The raven is mentioned two other times in the Bible as the special object of God's care (Job 38:41 and Psalm 147:9). We learn from this lesson that God cares for all creatures, however unattractive some of their habits may be.

Bible Insights

In this text Jesus forbade anxious thought or worry, but he did not order people to live in a reckless way. He advised his disciples to do their best and leave the rest to God. Because wealth in Palestine was often measured in the form of costly clothing that moths could ruin, Jesus told his listeners to imitate the lilies. If God cares for the birds and flowers, we should trust God to care even more for us. The Scripture offers an example of the theology of "enoughness"—the belief that God will provide what is needed for the physical life. Another example of this theology is the Old Testament story of the Hebrews who survived in the wilderness by gathering manna sufficient for only one day (Exodus 16).

Help the children understand that God's care includes a promise to provide all people with what they need to live. Worrying is not necessary. Our present and future is secure in God's hands.

Faith Nugget for Teachers

Our anxieties over food, clothing, and looks are unnecessary and futile.

BIBLE STUDY FOR TEACHER ENRICHMENT

TEACHING TIPS

The visual learner needs to see what you are teaching. By thinking in pictures or observing things closely, this learner will become impatient when having to listen for a long time. He or she prefers a neat classroom, has a vivid imagination, and may want to take notes or doodle. Teaching the visual learner means providing words, pictures, books, puppets, slides, videos, and bulletin boards for them to see. Write instructions on the board. Use charts and pictures to memorize verses.

STUDENT EXPERIENCE

Animals in the Bible:

```
Q U A I L L E Z A G Y
A P I G E O N S H E E
Y S P G M S N A K A N
E E T R A V E N T D O
M S N O C Z O L N S C
A H R A R O E V G N R
C E V O D K A L U A O
A E C O H R O W L K E
M P A R T R I D G E J
```

Beginning Moments

1. Greet children at the door as they arrive. Connect with their lives outside the classroom.

2. Check out displays. Invite the children to look at the display featuring pictures of animals and plants. Ask them to decide how God has equipped each one so that it is protected in nature. Examples: Porcupines have quills, rabbits can run, cactus plants have spines, trees have deep roots. Talk with the children about these creations of God.

3. Brainstorm about "worry." Have the children show worried looks on their faces. Ask the children to think of words that relate to worry. Write these words on the board. Examples might be: worry wart, Grandma or Grandpa, tests, worrier, death, afraid, the future, storms. Encourage many worry words or phrases. Leave these on the board to be erased at end of class.

Bible Story

1. Anticipate the Bible story. Show the children the Spiral Teaching Picture of the crown anemone and the raven. Share information about the nature items mentioned in the Bible Background and Insights.

If possible, go outside or to a sunny area for the Bible story. Sit on blankets, or go for a walk in an area with lots of birds and plants growing.

Before walking outside with the children, explain where you will go, how far, and what you will do there. Then <u>lead</u> the children rather than follow them.

2. Experience the Bible story. In the outdoor setting, ask the children to close their eyes while you recite or read the Scripture text. Tell the children to think of these words as coming directly from Jesus to each person. Speak with expression. Tell the story.

3. Wonder about the Bible story. After you have shared the Scripture story, offer thoughts like these:
- I wonder if Jesus was sitting in a patch of wildflowers when he talked to the disciples about worrying.
- I wonder if Jesus ever worried. When I worry, I often chew my fingernails or eat too much. (Teacher should include personal examples.) What do you do when you worry?
- I wonder what these words mean: "Of how much more value are you than the birds!" Am I more valuable than the birds? Is it okay to worry? What should I do when I am worried?
- I wonder when God has taken care of your worries. Would you like to tell about a time when God helped you stop worrying?

Invite thoughts or questions from the children.

Responses to the Bible Story

1. Act out the Bible story while you are still outside. Divide the children into three groups. Read or say the text while the children act it out. Have group one act out verses 22-23; group two does verses 24-26; group three does verses 27-28. For verses 29-32 the three groups come together and form a circle holding hands.

2. Confront worries. Return to the classroom. Choose one of the following activities:

a. Have a trained children's counselor talk with the children about worries and fears. (Inform the parents about this activity.) Be sensitive to specific fears that the children may have, such as death or divorce.

b. Hand out pieces of paper. Challenge children to sit quietly for one minute and to think about how they feel when they worry. After one minute tell the children to use lines, curves, colors, and shapes (and crayons) to depict their worries. After the first drawings are finished, the children complete second drawings in which they show God taking care of the worry. Give each child the freedom to decide what he or she will do with both drawings. (Some worriers may want to "give up" the worry by throwing it away. Others may want to confront it often and see it on the wall at home or in the classroom.)

3. Read in unison the memory passage from the Bible Memory Poster. Explain words that the children do not know. Point out the Bible memory text, "Do Not Worry," page 4, in the Student Leaflet. Explain that the Student Leaflet includes two translations of the same Scripture passage. The children will memorize only one translation during the quarter. Identify your preference so the children can memorize the same passage.

Closing Moments

1. Worship together. Help the children understand that all worries should be left to God.

a. Using the list of worries on the chalkboard (Beginning Moments #3), offer a class litany that repeats the phrase "Jesus says, 'Don't worry. God cares for you.' " Rephrase each word or group of words on your worry list. Then read each worry word or phrase and erase it. As you erase each word or phrase, the children say, "Jesus says, 'Don't worry. God cares for you.' "

b. Sing "Do Not Worry." Use the music cassette and song chart to help you.

c. Pray a prayer that asks God to flower or bloom in each child's heart so that there is no room for worrying.

2. Give each child a small flower (real, paper, plastic, or stitched) to remind him or her of God's constant care. Be sure the children take home the Student Leaflets.

BIBLE STORY

Jesus said to his disciples, "Therefore I tell you, do not worry about your life, what you will eat, or about your body, what you will wear. For life is more than food, and the body more than clothing.

"Consider the ravens; they neither sow nor reap, they have neither storehouse nor barn, and yet God feeds them. Of how much more value are you than the birds! And can any of you by worrying add a single hour to your span of life? If then you are not able to do so small a thing as that, why do you worry about the rest?

"Consider the lilies, how they grow: they neither toil nor spin; yet I tell you, even Solomon in all his glory was not clothed like one of these. But if God so clothes the grass of the field, which is alive today and tomorrow is thrown into the oven, how much more will he clothe you—you of little faith!

"And do not keep striving for what you are to eat and what you are to drink, and do not keep worrying. For it is the nations of the world that strive after all these things, and your Father knows that you need them. Instead, strive for his kingdom, and these things will be given to you as well.

"Do not be afraid, little flock, for it is your Father's good pleasure to give you the kingdom" (Luke 12:22-32).

Bible memory words
consider—to think about carefully
toil—to work hard and long
reap—to harvest a crop from a field
spin—to pull out and twist fiber into thread or yarn
Solomon—an Old Testament king who was wealthy and liked fine clothing
striving—trying to do something with serious effort

CHOICES

Use these ideas in place of or to supplement the session plan.

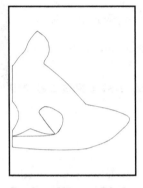

Do Not Worry Bird pattern

1. Read devotions. Share one or two stories from *Jellyfish Can't Swim and Other Secrets from the Animal World*, Marjorie Hodgson Parker (David C. Cook Publishing Co., 1991) or another children's devotional book.

2. Make nature rubbings. When you go outside for the Bible story, take along crayons and paper. Let the children rub crayons on paper placed on tree trunks and other large nature items. Small items like birds' feathers and grass blades can be taken into the classroom for rubbing. Remind the children that if God takes care of and plans the tiny details for each part of nature, God will also care for the details in each person's life.

3. Think about "enoughness." Jesus told the disciples not to worry about food or clothing. He advised them to be content with what they have. If Jesus talked to the "disciples" (class members) in this room today, what would he add to his list? What things do we have enough of? For example, "Do not worry about finding a place to live. Consider the turtle. It neither builds a house or rents one. Yet God houses it." Invite the children to brainstorm about additions to this Enoughness List. Write their suggestions on a poster board.

4. Make photograph verses. Help the children stage each verse for a photograph. Let the children determine how the verse would look if it were photographed. They can draw posters, make props or use real ones (you may need to provide these) to depict each verse in the Scripture passage. For example, verse 22 might show a girl with a worried expression looking at three cereal boxes and a boy with a worried expression looking at winter coats in a clothes catalog. You bring the camera and take a snapshot of each verse when the children are ready. Later in the quarter you may want to mount the photographs on a bulletin board or to show slides to the congregation for a Scripture reading.

5. Cut out Do Not Worry Birds. Use the pattern to make a Do Not Worry Bird. (See Resources, page 91.) First fold a 12 x 18 in., 30 x 45 cm., piece of construction paper in half. Lay the bird pattern on the fold. Trace and cut it out. Make a sample bird during class so the children can see how to do it. Allow time for the children to color the birds with crayons (or supply colored paper to represent kinds of birds—blackbird, bluejay, cardinal, brown thrush). After cutting, pull the end opposite the beak down and underneath the bird body, then over the neck of the bird so the wings spread out. Use thread, needles, and paper clips to hang birds from the classroom ceiling. Explain that these birds can remind children to trust in God.

To hang birds from a suspended ceiling, thread a needle and tie a knot at the end of the thread. Poke the needle through the top of the bird and pull the thread all the way through. Remove the needle and tie the other end of the thread onto a paper clip. Unfold the paper clip and hook it onto ceiling joints.

6. Write haiku (pronounced hī - kü) poetry. Follow the directions in the Student Leaflet for writing haiku poetry. To determine the number of syllables, the children should clap each part of the word.

Focus on nature and the ways God cares for animals and plants.

• Cut pictures of animals and plants out of nature magazines. Mount the pictures on the bulletin board or poster board. Have the children tell or write how God has equipped each one for its role in nature.

• Meet a plant. Go outside to an area with plantings. Let the children choose a plant or other specimen of nature to study for several minutes. Challenge them to "learn to know this friend."

• Gather for the Bible story. Read the Scripture text with enthusiasm.

• Worship together. Just as animals and plants have their own support systems, so do people. Ask the children to hold hands as you pray, seeking God's direction as children struggle with worries and fears. Sing "Do Not Worry."

• Make nature rubbings. Let the children create patterns with their rubbings.

• Return to the room to write a haiku. When the children are finished, they can use narrow-tip markers to print haiku on top of the nature rubbing.

3
TEACHING GRADE THREE

Focus on confronting worries.

• Brainstorm for "worry" words. If children struggle, ask them to think about things their parents, relatives, friends, or neighbors worry about. Add your own worry words so the children recognize that you too have similar problems.

• Discover Jesus' counsel. Together read Luke 12:22-31 from the children's Bibles.

• Wonder about the Bible passage. Discuss the children's understanding about the meaning and how the passage can help them.

• Listen to a trained counselor. (Be sure to inform the parents.)

• Make Do Not Worry Birds. Or cut two paper flowers for each child out of construction paper and write Luke 12:27 on each flower. One can be mounted on the bottom of the bulletin board. A second flower can be taken home.

• Capture worries. As you erase worry words from the board, let the children imagine capturing these worries between their hands. Lead a procession outside. Let the children offer these worries to God, open their hands, and the worries go. Close with prayer.

4
TEACHING GRADE FOUR

Focus on understanding the Bible passage.

• Brainstorm for worry words.

• Search for Jesus' advice about worrying. Hand out Bible concordances and ask the class to find where Jesus tells his disciples not to worry. Explain how to use a concordance. Have the children find the worry passage in two books of the New Testament (Matthew 6:25-34; Luke 12:22-31). Encourage group interaction. When they have found both references, turn to the Luke passage for further study.

• Hear Jesus' words. Read Luke 12:22-31 in unison.

• Wonder about the story. Help the children understand the biblical context of the passage. Help them learn that as Jesus' disciples today we have similar worries and fears.

• Stage photographs. Let the children choose verses to stage for slide pictures. Encourage them to retell the verses, and allow time for groups to plan and produce their verses. Let the children use a simple camera to take photos of other groups. Let the children work on puzzles in the Student Leaflet while they wait their turn to be photographed.

• Wipe away worries on the board. Worship together.

5
TEACHING GRADE FIVE

The Tables Are Turned

TEACHER PREPARATION

Find a helper
When you offer choices (Responses #1) ask a parent, other adult, or high school student to help. Be sure your helper understands what you expect of him or her.

Plan for Session 9
See Early Preparation #2, pages 58-59. Plan accordingly.

Student Leaflet Answers
Eighteen Tied-Up Words: DONKEY, WATER, HEALED, LEADER, HANDS, STRAIGHT, TEACHING, WONDERFUL, FREE, PRAISE, JESUS, WOMAN, SABBATH, SYNAGOGUE, MIRACLE, GOD, OX, STOOD.

Meditation

Great God, slacken the knots of my discipline and help me to lead the children in love and compassion. Remind me to teach as you taught and to bring to this lesson the kind of love that will empower your children to loving service.

Bible Scope

Luke 13:10-17

Bible Text

Luke 13:10-17

Bible Story Focus

When Jesus healed the crippled woman on the Sabbath, he taught that love for people is the most important law.

Bible Memory Passage

Luke 12:22-31 (25)

Faith Nugget for Children

One of the most important things we do is to love and help people.

Anticipated Outcomes

The children will feel a kinship with the woman who was healed, understand that loving others is at the core of Jesus' teachings, and feel motivated to respond to God.

Essential Supplies

•Resource Box: Spiral Teaching Picture Book, cassette, Bible Memory Poster, Bible Verse Visual

•Student Leaflets
•Tape player
•A smooth cloth or mat for moving the story figures
•Story figures (from the general classroom items) to represent Jesus, the woman, and the crowd
•A small block of wood to represent the synagogue
•Pieces of string or cord (1 yd./m. per child) tied to form a loop
•Animal halter or collar and a rope or leash
•Wire (4 ft./125 cm. lengths) that can be formed for wire sculptures—one per child, wire cutters or pliers
•4 x 4 x 1 in., 10 x 10 x 2.5 cm., wood pieces—one per child
•U-shaped tacks, hammer
•Bibles
•String cut in yard/meter lengths and tied to form a single loop—one per child
•*If you use any of the Choices, gather the appropriate supplies.*

Early Preparation

1. Practice string games. (See illustrations and Resources, page 93.)

2. Learn the Bible story of the crippled woman. Practice using the story figures.

3. Make a wire sculpture to show to the children (Responses #1b).

4. Learn the Bible memory verse, using sign language. (See Resources, pages 94-95, and Student Leaflet, p. 3.)

5. Put up the Spiral Teaching Picture in the worship center.

● ▽ ●

BIBLE STUDY FOR TEACHER ENRICHMENT

Bible Background

The cure of the crippled woman is recorded only in the Gospel of Luke. On the Sabbath, Jesus visited a synagogue in an unnamed village. While he was teaching there, he saw a woman who was probably suffering from an inflammatory disease of the bones that had caused her spinal joints to fuse together. Jesus' instantaneous cure contrasted sharply with her eighteen years of infirmity.

At this particular healing, Jesus stressed the welfare of the individual over obligations to religious laws. Jesus reasoned that if it was okay for one to care for household animals on the Sabbath, it was also okay to care for human infirmities on the Sabbath. The comparison between the release of the animals tied up with knots and the release of the woman whose backbone had been "knotted" makes the story work.

The woman who was healed immediately responded and began praising God. Her act of praise indicates an ongoing response. Luke chose the word *wonderful* to describe this healing. The gospels rarely use the word wonderful to describe one of Jesus' miracles. Truly, this healing was full of wonder.

Bible Insights

Jesus believed that people were more important than the religious laws of the day. Two other times he healed people on the Sabbath (Matthew 12:9-14 and Luke 14:1-6). In all these situations he was described as lord of the Sabbath.

Challenge the children always to look at people as children of God even when rules try to separate us from people. Challenge them to imitate Jesus' compassion and to develop attitudes of sympathy that will lead to acts of service. Challenge them always to put Jesus first in their lives.

Faith Nugget for Teachers

Sometimes even good rules can keep us from making God and people our priorities.

TEACHING TIPS

Use these ideas for moving the session along:

1. Start with a hands-on activity. Then do Bible memory or sharing time.

2. Ring a bell to call children to worship.

3. Set a kitchen timer so the children in groups know when their working or planning time is over.

4. Blink the lights two times. Then give instructions.

5. At the beginning of group work, say, "When you hear the music start, return to your seats and wait for instructions." Then play music at the appropriate time.

6. Set out supplies before class so you don't have to search for them during class time.

7. Have one or two children clean up a work area while you begin another activity with the rest of the class.

8. Compliment children who are ready for the next activity. Others will work quickly to finish up.

STUDENT EXPERIENCE:

String games

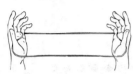

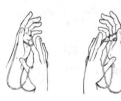

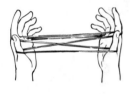

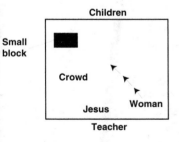

Bible story illustration

Beginning Moments

1. Greet the children at the door and hand each one a string for string games (Early Preparation #1). After children have a chance to show some of the string games they know, say that these games are related to a person in today's Bible story. Ask the children to move quietly to the worship center.

2. Sing "Asithi: Amen." (See Student Leaflet and Resource Box cassette.)

Bible Story

1. Anticipate the Bible story. Show the children a rope that could be used for tying up a horse, cow, or dog. Tell the children that today farmers use fences to keep animals from wandering. In Bible times the person who cared for an animal usually tied the animal to a tree, stake, or manger. The animal would be untied and led to get a drink of water. Every day of the week, several times a day the animal would need water. The farmer who cared about the animal would make certain that the animal got water regularly. Jesus uses the example of watering the ox and donkey to make an important point to a person who was criticizing him.

2. Experience the Bible story. [*Spread out the cloth. Add the block of wood and figures to represent the crowd. Place Jesus facing the crowd. See illustration.*] Tell the story.

3. Wonder about the Bible story. Offer these thoughts to the children:
• I wonder how Jesus felt about breaking the rules of the Pharisees. I wonder if it is okay to break the rules sometimes. What rules could be broken at home? at church? (shouting and running in church to warn people of a fire).
• I wonder who this woman was.
• I wonder how it felt to be healed.

Have you ever been healed by God? How did it feel? Do you know someone who was healed?

Responses to the Bible Story

1. After the story let the children choose one of these activities. They can form groups or work alone. Be flexible and tolerate more noise than usual.

a. Mime the story. Ask the children to study the Scripture passage from Luke 13:10-17; plan how the story will be retold, and present it using only actions.

b. Make wire sculptures. Let the children use wire to express how the woman must have felt when she was healed. Those working in a group might sculpt the main characters: woman, Jesus, Pharisee, and the crowd. Allow at least four feet/meters of wire for each sculpture and plenty of room to work. Tack the sculptures onto the square pieces of wood.

c. Compare the similarities and differences of the three Sabbath healings. Use the "Lord of the Sabbath" activity in the Student Leaflet. Be sure the children understand the instructions.

Allow ten to fifteen minutes for the activities.

2. Study the memory work together. Gather in a circle. Without speaking, form a sign for the Bible memory (Early Preparation #4). Indicate through gestures that the children should imitate you. Complete the entire Bible verse (25) in sign language; then ask the children if they know what you were telling them. Hand out Student Leaflets so children can practice sign language at home. (See Resources, p. 92.)

Closing Moments

1. Play *Human Pretzel*. Send two children out of the room. Instruct the

The illustration labels: Children, Small block, Crowd, Jesus, Woman, Teacher others to form a circle and while holding hands knot together by stepping over or under other hands. Tell circle members to keep a firm grip on their neighbor's hands. When the group is thoroughly knotted, bring the absent children back to unknot the circle. Before they start, tell them that they will have to wait until the next day because we can't do this work on Sunday (Sabbath). When the children object, tell them that helping people untangle their lives is more important than following a simple rule. Instruct those who left the room to begin work. When the circle is unknotted, the game is over. You can play again, using other people to untangle the circle.

2. Stand in a circle. Direct the children to stretch their arms out in front of them, cross their arms, and clasp hands with their neighbors. (See illustration.)

3. Pray together: "God, help us untangle the knots in our lives. We pray that you will help make us willing to love others as we are loved by God."

After the prayer the teacher lifts one arm over his or her head and turns to the outside. Still holding hands, each child in turn does the same until all face outward. Dismiss the class with the benediction "Go in love and peace. Amen."

One day a woman was walking near the synagogue in her village [*Hold woman figure at 45-degree angle to table*]. She was bent over—crippled as she had been for eighteen years [*Move woman to center*]. A crowd was gathered near the synagogue [*Touch heads of crowd*]. The woman thought she heard someone speak to her. When she looked around [*Woman turns toward Jesus*], she saw the man who had been teaching in the synagogue. He was talking to her. This was Jesus [*Point to Jesus*], the one many people had been talking about. This was Jesus [*Point to Jesus*], the one who had healed the sick. This was Jesus [*Point to Jesus*], the one who preached the good news. [*Put Jesus beside woman; point to Jesus*].

"Woman, you are set free from your ailment. You are healed," Jesus said.

[*Point to woman*] "What do you mean?" the woman asked.

[*Lift Jesus; tap on woman's head*] Then she felt the healing happen. The power from Jesus' hands went into her body, and she stood straight [*Woman stands straight*] for the first time in eighteen years. [*Point to woman*] "The pain is gone! The pain is gone!" she shouted. Then she began praising God. She went to everyone in the synagogue [*Move woman quickly to all people*]. "Thank you, God. Thank you, God. Praise God," the woman kept repeating.

When the leader of the synagogue saw what had happened [*Take figure from edge of crowd; set on block*], he was very angry because Jesus had healed the woman on the Sabbath. The leader spoke to the crowd [*Point to leader*], "There are six days on which work should be done; come on those days and be healed. Don't come on the Sabbath day."

[*Point to Jesus*] "Do you untie your donkey on the Sabbath and lead it to water?"

[*Point to leader*] "Yes."

[*Point to Jesus*] "Do you see this woman whose back has been tied up for eighteen long years?"

[*Point to leader*] "Yes."

[*Point to Jesus*] "Shouldn't her back be set free on the Sabbath day?"

The synagogue leader and others who did not like Jesus felt bad [*Leader and three others walk away, backs turned*]. But everyone else was excited and delighted that the woman was healed [*Lift figures slightly to indicate joy*]. They rejoiced for this healing and about all the other wonderful things that Jesus was doing [*Point to Jesus*]. Praise God! Praise God! Praise God!

CHOICES

Use these ideas in place of or to supplement the session plan.

Instructions for folding Sonburst tie-dye

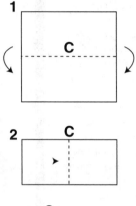

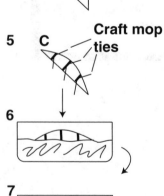

Craft mop ties

Sonburst

1. Tie knots. As an opening activity, provide ropes and practice tying a variety of knots.

2. String the story along. Tell the story using a string trick that you are very familiar with. Add a detail to the trick as you tell each important part of the story. At the punch line—either when the woman is healed or when the crowd rejoices—reach a point in the string trick when the string becomes just a string again. (See Resources, p. 93.)

3. Sing praise songs. If you do not like to lead singing, ask a song leader to assist you. Allow ten minutes for singing.

4. Design get-well cards. Draw pictures for church friends who are in the hospital. Provide envelopes for the children to address.

5. Make "Sonbursts" with tie-dye. Purchase white cotton handkerchiefs, craft mop (or other wide string), and fabric dye. (See illustrations.) Fold as shown. Tie craft mop around handkerchiefs in wide strips. Knot. Dip handkerchiefs in dye. Follow directions for fabric dye. After the allotted time, dip handkerchiefs in cold water to set dye. When Sonbursts are dry, unknot. Notify parents ahead of time so children can dress accordingly. Supply paint shirts to catch splatters.

6. Resolve to live peaceably by helping each other and working together. Another meaning for untie is to clear up or resolve. During a discussion time, talk about conflicts that have been resolved between countries or parts of nations. Make clear the idea that God wants us to live in harmony with other people. One way to do that is to help others.

7. Lace up relationships. Partners stand side by side and tie together laces of adjoining shoes (similar to gunnysack races). Challenge the children to walk around together. Then explain that when we help people, we often must "walk" closely with them until they are able to help themselves.

• ▽ • • • •

• Play string games (Beginning Moments #1).

• Sing praise songs, including "Asithi: Amen" in the Student Leaflet. Let the children play simple rhythm instruments like wood blocks or finger symbols.

• Tell the story using a string game. Assume an omniscient (all-knowing) point of view. Wonder about the story.

• Freeze the action. Read Luke 13:10-17 from the Bible—sentence by sentence. At the end of each sentence, say "freeze." Children assume character

positions as if taken by a still camera. After children have "frozen" into place, allow a brief "thawing" time before reading the next sentence.

• Design get-well cards. Have the children use black, fine-tip markers so designs can be photocopied and sent regularly to church members who are ill.

• Discuss conflict resolution.

• Tie shoelaces together (Choices #7).

• Worship in pairs. Have the children say the Bible memory verse to each other and offer a prayer thanking God for their partner.

3
TEACHING GRADE THREE

• ▽ • • • • • •

• Learn to tie knots in ropes. (Check an encyclopedia for examples.) Explain to the children that sometimes our lives seem to be "tied up." Jesus is the one who can untie the knots.

• Sing and worship together.

• Tell the story from the woman's point of view. Wonder about the story.

• Offer options for Responses to the Bible Story: (a) Make wire sculptures of

characters in the story. Purchase flexible wire in a hardware store or recycle wire from spiral notebooks. (b) Study the three Sabbath healings. (See the Student Leaflet for instructions.) (c) Write and present news for RADIO J-E-S-U-S. Feature the news story of the woman's healing. Include brief news reports from previous lessons.

• End with Closing Moments #2 and #3.

4
TEACHING GRADE FOUR

• ▽ • • • • • •

• Make Sonbursts (Choices #5). If each child completes two, they can be sewn together on three sides, stuffed with cotton filling, stitched shut, and given as gifts.

• Tell the Bible story from the woman's point of view.

• Wonder about the story. Discuss contemporary conflicts in the news. Use magazine or newspaper articles to clarify the discussion for children. Recognize that solutions to problems are very complex, but challenge chil-

dren to question injustices wherever they are and to seek God's perfect guidance in all issues.

• Untie scrambled words. Have the children do "Eighteen Tied-Up Words" in the Student Leaflet. Ask children to explain the meaning of the title (eighteen is the number of years the woman suffered from her disease).

• Worship together, praying silent prayers.

5
TEACHING GRADE FIVE

9 Only One Boss

TEACHER PREPARATION

Meditation

Daily I struggle as I make decisions, O Lord God. The children in my class struggle with decisions too. Some decisions are easy; some are not. Many choices are good ones but not always the best choices. Once again I commit my life to you, and I ask for your spirit-filled presence as I plan and teach the lesson.

Bible Scope

Luke 14:15-24; 16:10-13

Bible Text

Luke 14:15-24; 16:10-13

Bible Story Focus

Jesus taught that the disciples had to choose between serving God or serving things.

Bible Memory Passage

Luke 12:22-31 (26)

Faith Nugget for Children

Jesus calls us to commit ourselves to God everyday.

Anticipated Outcomes

The children will understand the Bible's teachings about serving God and will want to follow Jesus daily.

Essential Supplies

- Resource Box: Spiral Teaching Picture Book, cassette, Bible Memory Poster, Bible Verse Visual

- Student Leaflets
- Tape recorder
- A soft cloth or mat for telling the story
- Story figures to represent the man giving the banquet, servants, and guest (general classroom items)
- A miniature table or box to represent a table
- Mini road signs (Beginning Moments #1 and Closing Moments #2)
- Costume or head tie for storyteller (Bible Story)
- Lightweight poster board cut in pieces 2 x 2 in., 5 x 5 cm.
- Markers or crayons
- Pictures of traffic signs or driving handbook showing road signs (Closing Moments #2)
- *If you use any of the Choices, gather the appropriate supplies.*

Early Preparation

1. Prepare a mini road sign for each child to wear. Signs read "I will turn to Christ."

2. Decide whether to have a driving or walking tour for the "On the Road" activity (Responses #1). If you use vans or cars, be sure seat belts are available for every passenger. Drive the possible route once, looking for road signs you can point out to the children. Look for service opportunities such as areas that need trash picked up.

3. Secure written permission from parents or guardians for the "On the Road" experience. During the week send notes that briefly describe the activity, date, and suggestions for appropriate dress. Include a permission slip (with place for parental signature) for the children to return signed. Have available extra permission slips for visitors and children who may forget.

4. Set up the Spiral Teaching Picture Book in the worship center.

5. Learn the song "The Wedding Banquet." (See Resource Box cassette.) Words are printed on page 60 in this guide.

● ▽ ●

Bible Background

Unlike workers today who can hold two or more jobs for several different employers, the slave in Jesus' parable would have worked from sunup to sundown for only one master. Total devotion was essential.

Different Bible translations and commentaries refer to the parable in Luke 14 in a variety of ways: a king's banquet, great banquet, great feast, great dinner, or great supper. To understand this parable, take note of these cultural understandings. In Palestine when a feast was prepared, the host sent invitations a long time before the feast, and the guests accepted or declined the invitation at that time. The hour of the feast was not announced until the feast day when servants were sent out to summon the guests. Declining this "time to eat" announcement was considered extremely rude.

In the parable the master stood for God, and the invited guests represented the Jews who had waited through history for the Messiah. But when they were finally offered God's invitation, they refused. The street people represented those who welcomed Jesus; the road people were the Gentiles.

The first two guests declined because of business dealings, but their excuses were rather weak. Usually fields are inspected *before* they are purchased. The farmer with the five yoke of oxen most likely owned a large piece of land. Anyone with such wealth would have had servants to do the work.

The third guest referred to ancient Jewish law which excused a newly married man for one year from all military duties and other business (Deuteronomy 24:5).

Bible Insights

Choices. That's what this lesson is about. Children can choose to answer the call of God or to respond to other calls. The Parable of the Great Dinner dishes up a story that reminds us to follow Christ at the moment we are called. It helps us remember that as Christians we continue to make choices when we follow Christ.

Faith Nugget for Teachers

Many things can distract us from our commitment and our allegiance to God.

BIBLE STUDY FOR TEACHER ENRICHMENT

TEACHING TIPS

Teachers sometimes feel alone in their teaching. To avoid that lonely feeling, invite a family member of each child to help you for one session. Such regular support will lessen teacher burnout and create bonds between you and the families of your children. In this session, for example, adults can drive while you talk, search for books on servanthood, bring a favorite pet, tell the story, or cut paper for comic strips. Assign child helpers based on whose family member is helping you each week.

STUDENT EXPERIENCE

The Wedding Banquet

Solo: I cannot come. I cannot come to the banquet, don't trouble me now. I have married a wife. I have bought me a cow. I have fields and commitments that cost a pretty sum. Pray, hold me excused, I cannot come.
1. A certain man held a feast on his fine estate in town. He laid a festive table and wore a wedding gown. He sent invitations to his neighbors far and wide but when the meal was ready, each of them replied: (Repeat solo)
2. The master rose up in anger, called his servants by name, said: "Go into the town, fetch the blind and the lame, fetch the peasant and the pauper for this I have willed, my banquet must be crowded, and my table must be filled." (Repeat solo)
3. When all the poor had assembled, there was still room to spare, so the master demanded: "Go search ev'rywhere, to the highways and the byways and force them to come in. My table must be filled before the banquet can begin. (Repeat solo)
Words and music: Miriam Therese Winter, Copyright: Medical Mission Sisters, 1965. Used by permission.

Plan ahead. *Ask a child to bring a favorite Christian music tape to use in class next week.*

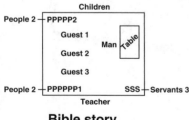

Bible story illustration

Beginning Moments

1. Greet the children at the classroom door. Collect permission slips. Have your helper try to get signatures for visitors and children who may have forgotten.

2. Pin a mini road sign on each child (Early Preparation #1). Encourage the children to work in small groups to learn the Bible memory verse or play the ACTS game from the Resource Box.

3. Play *Follow the Leader.* Assign two children to be the leaders. After each leader has had a turn to lead the group, challenge the children to follow both leaders at the same time. Try this in the classroom with simple hand or arm actions, or go outside and use more traditional actions. Some actions can be done simultaneously (for example, hopping and nodding head); others cannot (running and walking). Change leaders if you wish, but do not allow more than five to ten minutes for the activity. Discuss briefly the difficulty of following more than one leader.

4. Tell the children to follow your actions. Visibly close your mouth and move very slowly and quietly to the Bible story area.

Bible Story

1. Anticipate the Bible story. Sing "The Wedding Banquet" (Early Preparation #5).

2. Experience the Bible story. [*Spread out the cloth. Set the table on one side of the cloth. Have the story figures handy.*] Say, "Here is a story that Jesus told." Tell the story.

3. Wonder about the Bible story. After the story allow a time for thinking about the story as you make these or similar comments:
• I wonder what the people who heard this story thought.
• I wonder why the people in the story didn't want to eat at the man's house. Are there times when we don't want to go places where we are invited? What kinds of excuses do we use? Is it okay to make up an excuse?
• I wonder how the poor people who were invited felt.
• I wonder if Jesus was talking about heaven. Are there people today who always say no to God? I wonder what God is asking me to do that I should say yes to.

Responses to the Bible Story

1. Spend most of the rest of the lesson "on the road" if weather allows. Use the sidewalks/roads near your church to teach the children about making choices. Walk or drive, and let the children decide when you will turn and which direction to go. When they ask, "Where are we going?" say, "I don't know. Where should we be going?" After about five or ten minutes, explain that if we do not have Christ as our guide, we don't know where our lives are headed, and we may choose to go the wrong way. End this activity with prayers of dedication that use road/street images. For example, "As I follow you on the road of life, O God, remind me to stop and help people who need you."

2. Look for opportunities for a class service project as you head back to church. Let the children think of the ideas and help them focus on a project that is appropriate for their age. Help children realize that often we must intentionally choose to serve Christ. Serving is one way we can show God that we are followers.

Closing Moments

1. Return to the classroom and complete plans for the service project. Allow the children to accept full ownership of the project and offer to manage tasks they assign to you.

2. Let children redesign traffic signs that will tell others to choose Christ. For example, YIELD TO CHRIST. Post them on the classroom door as children leave class.

3. Remind the children to use their Jerusalem Moments Calendar, that you sent home at the beginning of the quarter, for daily devotions. Ask them to tell you next Sunday what their favorite activity was for this week.

4. Say a word of blessing to each child as you dismiss them. Be sure they take home the Student Leaflets.

BIBLE STORY

[*Point to man*] Here is a man who planned a great dinner. "I'm planning a delicious feast, and I've invited many people." The servants helped him make all the preparations [*Servants enter one by one, touch table, and exit*]. The special day arrived. The man looked around at the meal the servants had prepared [*Point to man*]. "I've planned a delicious feast. Now it is time to call the guests who have been invited." The man summoned one of his servants [*Enter servant, point to man*]. "Go to all the people I've invited. Tell them to come."

[*Move servant to guest 1; point to servant*] "Come. Everything is ready."

[*Guest 1 faces away from servant*] "I can't come. I've just bought some land, and I must go see it. Please excuse me" [*Guest 1 exits, move servant to guest 2*].

The servant went to the second invited guest. "Come. Everything is ready."

[*Guest 2 faces away from servant*] "I can't come. I have bought five yoke of oxen, and I must go try them out. Please excuse me" [*Guest 2 exits, move servant to guest 3*].

The servant went to the third invited guest. "Come. Everything is ready."

[*Guest 3 faces away from servant*] "I can't come. I just got married. Please excuse me" [*Guest 3 exits, servant goes to master*].

The servant went back and reported everything to his master. Then the master got angry. He said to the servant, "Go out to the streets and alleys of the town and bring in the people who have no money and the people who can't see and the people who can't walk."

[*Servant goes to people 1; some walk to table, others are carried*] The servant did that, but there was room for many more.

[*Point to man*] "Go back out to the country roads and make them come in. I want my house full. I tell you, not one of the people I invited will get a taste of my banquet" [*Servant goes to people 2; all go to places at table*].

CHOICES

Use these ideas in place of or to supplement the session plan.

Choices
Everyday
My choices
Tell others
What I think
About God.

1. Invite a well-trained dog (or other well-trained pet) and the pet's owner to Sunday school for the first five to ten minutes of class. Use the pet's presence to help the children learn about responding with devotion to a supreme being. (The pet should be well-trained and thoroughly devoted to its owner. The owner should be kind and loving to the pet.) Arrange for this visit early in the week. Ask the person to show or tell how the pet responds to a devoted friend. Limit this invitation to only one animal. Be sensitive to children with fears or allergies.

2. Let the children retell the Bible story with the story figures. They may use the story in the Student Leaflet or create their own dialogue.

3. Play *Kids' Choices*. This is a commercial game (available in Christian bookstores) that applies biblical principles to everyday situations (Rainfall, Inc., 1988). Or use the situations on the cards to provide discussion-starters.

4. Draw comic strips of the Parable of the Great Dinner. Drawing space is available in the Student Leaflet. Show comic strips from the newspaper. Explain that only important details are shown. Balloons for speech are drawn and read from left to right. Offer pencils, pens, or colored pencils.

Write four ideas on the board to get children started. Encourage a realistic interpretation of the story, but for those children who often think in comedy, allow the humorous side of the story to come through.

5. Use a modern-day point of view for the comic strips. For example:

Frame 1: Come to my house for pizza.

Frame 2: Can't come. Just bought some bubble gum … turned on the TV … changed the calendar.

Frame 3: My neighbors won't come. I'll invite interstate travelers.

Frame 4: (sign on billboard) Free pizza. Next right.

6. Find stories of Christians who have faithfully followed Christ. Provide stories that you can offer to the children for reading at home or let them find books in the church library. One option is *Ted Studebaker: A Man Who Loved Peace* by Joy Hofacker Moore (Herald Press, 1987).

7. Play the *ACTS* game from the Resource Box. (See Resources, page 92, for directions.)

• Invite a pet. Ask someone who visits frequently in homes to recommend a church member who owns a well-trained dog or other pet. Use this animal to call attention to the responsiveness of Christians to their Master.

• Let the children use the story figures (Choices #2). The story may be new for most of the children, so you should explain that the parable is one that Jesus told. Wonder about the story.

• Do your own walking tour for the "On the Road" activity. Allow only five minutes for this activity.

• Plan a service project. Suggest that children think of projects that they and their parents or other adults in the church can do together.

• Let children choose one of the following:

a. Read the poem "Choices" in Student Leaflet. Write poems about decisions.

b. Make bumper stickers that remind people to make wise choices.

c. Do the "Road Sign Order" puzzle in the Student Leaflet.

• Worship together. Sing, pray, and repeat the Bible memory verse.

3
TEACHING GRADE THREE

• Spend the entire class period out of the classroom.

• Choose to play. Play *Follow the Leader* outside, using traditional actions.

• Be mobile. Tell the Bible story in your car or van and then walk or drive as children guide the decision making during "On the Road."

• Choose to serve. Plan a service activity as you are seated together in a vehicle. Ask for a volunteer to write suggestions on a sheet of paper. Ask for another volunteer to lead the discussion.

• Worship together. Sing favorite songs and repeat the Bible memory verse. Pray together.

• Choose to read. End the session in the church library or around a table of books (of varying reading levels) that focus on faithful service to Christ. A librarian can help you find suitable ones for the readers in your class. Let the children check out several books. Encourage them to choose books or stories that can help them make the right choices either now or later in life.

4
TEACHING GRADE FOUR

• Play *Double Leader*. Rename *Follow the Leader* so older children don't immediately associate it as a childish game. Sit around the work table and use only simple head and arm movements.

• Add depth to the story. Use details explained in Bible commentaries to add realism to "The Parable of the Great Dinner." To hold the interest of children who know the story well, include details from the Bible Background.

• Offer children three options or learning centers:

a. Do "Kids' Choices"—for the thinkers/talkers (Choices #3).

b. Draw comic strips in the Student Leaflet or on large poster board—for the artists (Choices #4 or #5).

c. Read books or stories of faithful Christians—for the seekers (Choices #6). Stories from the *Martyrs Mirror* may be appropriate for some classes.

• Worship together. Sing favorite songs, pray, and repeat as much of the Bible memory passage as the children can remember.

5
TEACHING GRADE FIVE

10 God Judges Our Acts

TEACHER PREPARATION

Student Leaflet Answers
Like the Flowers: Consider how the lilies grow. They do not labor or spin. Yet I tell you, not even Solomon in all his splendor was dressed like one of these (Luke 12:27, NIV).

Plan ahead for Session 11
Invite parents or adult church friends of the children to come for next week's session. Be sure each child will have an adult present. Ask adults to be sure that each child brings a baby photograph and a favorite baby toy. (See Session 11 Early Preparation, p. 70.)

Plan ahead for Session 12
Obtain tax information. (See Early Preparation, p. 76.)

Meditation
When you judge my life, Almighty God, please look at my heart and my deeds. Accept the weekly offering I make as I teach the lessons of your love and faithfulness. I am devoted to you, O God. May the kindnesses of my heart show that devotion.

Bible Scope
Luke 16:19-31

Bible Text
Luke 16:19-31

Bible Story Focus
Jesus told the story of a rich man, punished for his greed and lack of compassion. The man's actions are contrasted with God's love for needy Lazarus.

Bible Memory Passage
Luke 12:22-31 (27)

Faith Nugget for Children
God wants us to show kindness without playing favorites.

Anticipated Outcomes
The children will affirm each other and experience Christ's teaching about kindness.

Essential Supplies
• Resource Box: Spiral Teaching Picture Book, cassette, Bible Memory Poster, Bible Verse Visual

• Student Leaflet
• Tape player
• Music cassette for Beginning Moments #3
• Unsliced bread
• Balloons and/or crepe paper to decorate Hot Seat
• Lily or other flower
• *If you use any of the Choices, gather the appropriate supplies.*

Early Preparation
1. Remind the children you asked last week to bring a cassette tape of their favorite Christian music.

2. Practice telling the story using the suggested instructions. Record yourself so you can hear what the children will hear.

3. Write instructions for Beginning Moments #2 on the chalkboard or chart paper.

4. Arrange two rows of chairs (one per child minus one) back to back.

5. Decorate the Hot Seat (Responses #1).

6. Write role-play situations on slips of paper.

7. Set up the Spiral Teaching Picture Book in the worship center.

● ▽ ●

BIBLE STUDY FOR TEACHER ENRICHMENT

Bible Background

The Parable of the Rich Man and Lazarus uses the literary technique known as irony to teach the lesson on judgment. The theme is similar to the blessings on the poor and woes on the rich in Luke 6. The use of irony was common in storytelling in Jesus' day. This is a parable on judgment and should not be viewed as an accurate guide to the next world.

In all of Jesus' parables Lazarus was the only person mentioned by name. The name means "God helps." The rich man is often called Dives, the Latin word for "rich." Although Lazarus was a weak and hungry beggar, he was, in God's eyes, important enough to feast with Abraham in paradise.

The rich man did not escape the consequences of his uncaring attitude on earth. He suffered eternal punishment. Every phrase in the parable adds significant meaning to the character of this self-centered, pompous, authoritative, rich man. The man wore purple outer garments and fine linen undergarments, clothing similar to that of the high priests. He feasted daily on expensive gourmet foods, wiping his hands on hunks of bread, as was the custom of the times. These pieces of bread were the ones thrown out and eaten by beggars and unclean animals like dogs.

Bible Insights

Help the children understand that the contrast between the poor man and the rich man should not be interpreted that wealth is bad and poverty is good. Such an interpretation would complicate the meaning. Help the children recognize that the rich man ended up in hell because he did not care about anyone but himself. In contrast, the poor man was content with his life on earth and trusted God. God had a place for the poor man in heaven with the leaders of the faith.

Faith Nugget for Teachers

God judges us on the basis of the way we treat others and the way we respond to what life offers us.

TEACHING TIPS

The story will prompt questions about heaven and hell. Be prepared for the children's questions. If there are some questions you cannot answer, assure the children you will try to find out more information. Explain that there are some things about heaven and hell that we don't know. Follow through. Show that you value their questions.

STUDENT EXPERIENCE

Beginning Moments

1. Welcome each child at the door with a kind word, a sincere compliment, or a gentle pat on the back.

2. Direct the children's attention to your written instructions: WRITE THE NAMES OF PEOPLE GOD WANTS YOU TO BE KIND TO. Challenge the children to fill the board or chart paper with names or groups of people. Encourage them to work together and help each other. (Save this list. You will use the names during Closing Moments.)

3. Play *Musical Chairs*—with a bias. Direct the children to a row of chairs set back to back—one chair less than the number of children. Use the following pattern until only one child is left:

    a. Start the tape-recorded music.

    b. After a short time, stop the music.

    c. Children should sit down.

    d. The child who does not have a chair is eliminated.

    e. Remove one chair from the circle. (*Repeat these steps*)

At the end of the activity, discuss the feelings they had while they played this game.

Ask the children who were eliminated to tell how they felt. Encourage them to express their feelings of disappointment of being left out, of thinking they failed. Explain that in our world some individuals are left out because of how they look, where they live, how they think, how much money they have, and other reasons.

Bible Story

1. Anticipate the Bible story. Ask children to move quietly to the story/worship center. On the Spiral Teaching Picture, point to the word PARABLE. Remind the children that Jesus often told stories. These stories were called parables. They taught lessons through everyday objects and situations.

Show children large portions of unsliced bread. Explain that in Bible times people did not use forks, knives, spoons, or napkins. After eating, they wiped their hands on hunks of bread and threw them out. Usually the pieces of bread were eaten by animals, but sometimes hungry, poor people would eat the pieces too. One story Jesus told was about a poor person named Lazarus who depended for his food on bread thrown out by a rich man.

2. Experience the Bible story. Say, "The name of this story is the 'Parable of the Rich Man and Lazarus.' Jesus told this story to his disciples" [*Use the few actions indicated. Avoid the "up" of heaven and "down" of hell*]. Tell the story.

3. Wonder about the Bible story. Use these wondering statements to initiate questions children have about the story:

•I wonder why the rich man ignored Lazarus when they were both living.

•I wonder how Lazarus felt when the rich man ignored him.

•I wonder how it felt for Lazarus to be in heaven with Abraham.

•I wonder what I could do to help people like Lazarus. Are there some people you know who are left out?

•I wonder what Jesus meant when he said, "Where your treasure is, there your heart will be also." What did you learn when you asked an adult about this during the week? Invite responses to "Think About This" in last week's Student Leaflet.

Responses to the Bible Story

1. Point to the Hot Seat, a chair decorated with balloons and crepe paper. Tell children that all of them (including the teacher) will have the opportunity to sit in the Hot Seat. Explain its purpose: One person sits in the Hot Seat while classmates and teacher tell (or write) what they like about the person or what the person does well. Remind them that all comments must be positive and genuine. The activity serves two purposes: Children feel good about giving genuine compliments, and they also feel good when people compliment them. Separate large classes into groups of five or six.

Together say a prayer for each child after he or she receives the compliments. Incorporate the compliment into the prayer.

2. Explain that role-plays can help us understand others. Hand out slips of paper with the following situations (or make up your own). Allow a few minutes for children to form groups and plan their role-playing situations. Then ask each group to tell the class about their problem and to act out their solutions. Accept a variety of responses as long as they show kindness.

If children have difficulty with this activity, ask questions to help them establish each character:

Who are you?

What happened?

What kinds of problems are you having?

What do you think you should do?

•(three people) Sandee wears the same clothes every day of the week. While two people are talking about her, Sandee overhears. How does she respond? (Be sensitive. If this situation fits someone in your class, choose another situation.)

•(three people) During a ball game a teammate makes a bad play. Mario hears his friends talking about the teammate. What does he say?

•(two people) On their way to a baby-sitting job, Amanda and a relative accidentally break part of a fence belonging to Amanda's neighbor. What do they do?

3. Show the children a lily (or another kind of flower) to help them memorize "Consider the lilies..." (Luke 12:27). Explain that Solomon was a king in the Old Testament who had much wealth and could dress in the very best clothes. Read the verse from the Bible Memory Poster several times with the children.

<hr>

BIBLE STORY

[*Use pompous voice*] There was once a very rich man who was so wealthy that he dressed in the finest purple cloth and wore undergarments made of the finest linen. Every day of the week this rich man feasted on the finest foods, and every day of the week [*Lift up unsliced bread*] he used lots of bread to wipe his hands after he ate [*Wipe hands with bread and drop used pieces of bread on the floor*].

[*Weak voice*] At the rich man's gate lay a very poor man whose name was Lazarus. Sores covered his body, and he was so helpless that he couldn't even drive away the dogs who came to lick his sores. His only food was the small pieces of bread that the rich man had used to wipe his hands [*Point to bread on the floor*].

[*Normal voice*] When the poor man died, he was carried away by the angels to be with Abraham and to feast at Abraham's table in heaven. The rich man also died. He looked from his place in hell where he was being tormented and saw Abraham far away with Lazarus by his side.

The rich man begged Abraham to take away the torment of the afterlife. Abraham reminded the rich man of his life on earth. During the rich man's life on earth, he had ignored the needs of people. Now he was suffering the consequences.

But during Lazarus' time on earth, he had patiently accepted his poor life. His reward was eternity in heaven [*Quietly clean up bread and bread crumbs*].

<hr>

Encourage them to read it from their Bibles and say it everyday at home.

4. Sing together "Let Me Be Your Servant, Jesus." Use the cassette to help you learn the song. The words and music are printed in the Student Leaflet for Session 13. Sing "Seek Ye First the Kingdom of God." (See Resource Box cassette.)

5. Ask the children to share their favorite activity from the Jerusalem Moments Calendar. (See Session 9 Closing Moments #3.) Encourage them to use their calendar during the coming week.

Closing Moments

1. Do a kindness cheer. Gather the children near you on the floor and ask them to think of people God wants them to be kind to (Beginning Moments #2). Make your hand into a fist (to indicate strength in kindness). Put your fist on the floor as you name an individual or group of persons to whom you can be kind.

For example: Lynn, my teacher, the homeless, new people in our church. The children stack their hands on yours one by one. As they do so, they name someone to whom God wants them to be kind. Encourage shouting of the names in a cheer fashion to indicate that kindness can be fun. Move hands from the bottom of the pile to the top, and continue the cheer until the children can no longer reach the top. Then all shout AMEN to end the kindness cheer-prayer.

2. Play *Musical Chairs*—unbiased. Have the children help put the chairs in a circle (one per child). Direct the children to sit on the chairs. Start the music and ask the children to walk around the inside of the circle. Remove a chair while the children walk. When the music stops, the child without a chair sits on another player's lap, holds hands with or in some way stays connected to the player. Continue playing the music and removing chairs until all players are seated on or connected in some way to the one remaining chair. At the end of the game, compare the single chair to the world and explain that in order to live at peace with everyone who shares the earth, we must treat all people with kindness.

3. Dismiss the children with a boisterous AMEN similar to the completion of the kindness cheer. Be sure they take home their Student Leaflets.

CHOICES

1. Show the children a boomerang during Opening Moments and ask if they have ever used one or seen one used. When thrown, the boomerang returns to the thrower. Hand out cross boomerangs (see pattern) made from thin cardboard. Show the children how to balance the boomerang on the ends of the fingertips and flick it off the fingers. After a few minutes of play, explain that something like a boomerang happens in today's story. (Do unto others as you want God to do unto you. Our goodness helps others and returns to us to make us happy.)

Boomerang Crosses
Enlarge these patterns. Cut crosses out of lightweight cardboard. Use the smaller pattern in small rooms, the larger pattern in large areas.
Idea adapted from test congregation Foothills Mennonite Church, Calgary, Alberta.

2. Before telling the story, hand out large pieces of drawing paper and encourage children to draw the story as they hear it being told. Their feelings about the story will show in their drawings. Later you can discuss their concerns about heaven and hell. Tell the story more than once, or have them find it in the Bible so they can gather details.

3. As a class, interview one or two adults in your church congregation who exemplify kindness. Ask your pastor to recommend someone if you do not know the congregation well.

4. Prepare a quick-bread recipe (like the crumb muffins in the Student Leaflet) in class and share the finished bread with someone who needs some extra kindness.

5. Discuss prejudice as related to your country's or community's history. Give examples of ways Anabaptists and Friends have tried to thwart prejudice (for example, early mission work among Native people).

6. Let the children use the story figures to retell the story.

7. Have the children design book jackets for the Gospel of Luke. (See Student Leaflet.)

•Play *Musical Chairs*—with a bias. For large classes, occasionally eliminate more than one chair at a time to move the game along.

•Discuss prejudice. One meaning of the word is to pre-judge, which implies that full understanding is missing before one makes a decision. Most prejudice refers to irrational hate against a group of people.

•Hand out drawing papers.

•Tell the Bible story. Encourage children to draw the story as you tell it a second time.

•Let children share their drawings.

•Hand out cross boomerangs (Choices #1). Instruct the children to write the name of a person that they want to be kind to during the next week on the boomerang.

•Sit in a circle of chairs for worship. Lay the crosses on the floor in a cross pattern. Pray "Help us to be kind, O God. Help us to be loving, O God. Help us to be like you, O God."

•Play *Musical Chairs*—unbiased (Closing Moments #2).

3
TEACHING GRADE THREE

••• ▽ •••••

•If you have a small group, spend the entire session in the church kitchen or bring mixing supplies to the classroom.

•Prepare a quick-bread recipe with the children. Assign children to add ingredients. Ask an adult to monitor the baking while you continue the session. If time allows, wrap the cooled products for gift-giving.

•Have the children name people to whom we should be kind.

•Tell the story as you clean up the kitchen together. Encourage the children to ask questions (in the natural way friends visit in a kitchen). As you work, talk about prejudice, heaven and hell, or relationships. Follow the leading of the children—meet them where they are in their Christian walk—without offering simplistic answers.

•Worship together near the finished quick breads.

•Deliver the quick-bread gifts.

4
TEACHING GRADE FOUR

••• ▽ •••••

•As the children arrive, hand each one a slip of paper. Instructions read: TAKE A CANDY FROM THE DISH ON THE TABLE. Have a dish of candy nearby and observe what happens. One person's paper is blank. Ignore that person while you briefly visit with the others.

•Gather together and discuss how it feels to be left out or ignored. Why are people left out? How can we help someone who is ignored? Be sure the child who was left out feels included.

•Read the poem about Lazarus on page 1 of the Student Leaflet.

•Read the Bible text from Luke 16:19-31. Wonder about the Bible story.

•Put children on the Hot Seat. Writing compliments rather than saying them may be easier for this age. Plan what you will say or write about each child.

•Have the children act like the people in the role-play situations (Responses #2).

•Discuss prejudice in your country's or community's history. If necessary, do research to help you explain problems or situations to the children. Be sensitive to minorities in your class.

•Worship together.

5
TEACHING GRADE FIVE

Jubilee Is for Children

TEACHER PREPARATION

Meditation

Just as you welcomed the children to your loving heart, O God of all beings, let me also draw the children close to me. May all my actions, words, and thoughts reflect your love.

Bible Scope

Luke 18:15-17

Bible Text

Luke 18:15-17

Bible Story Focus

The disciples tried to keep the children from Jesus, but he said, "The kingdom belongs to the children."

Bible Memory Passage

Luke 12:22-31 (28)

Faith Nugget for Children

As children, we are important to Jesus.

Anticipated Outcomes

The children will celebrate their own early childhoods and recognize their importance to the church body.

Essential Supplies

•Resource Box: Spiral Teaching Picture Book, music cassette, Bible Memory Poster, Bible Verse Visual

•Student Leaflets
•Tape player
•Story figures from the general classroom items (entire set)
•Name tags and pens
•Writing paper and pencils or poster board/newsprint and markers
•Pan of finger paint or stamp pad
•*If you use any of the Choices, gather the appropriate supplies.*

Early Preparation

1. Invite parents or adult church friends of the children to come for the entire class period.

2. Ask the children to each bring a photo showing them at about age one and a favorite toy from that age. If your class has irregular attendance, ask only one child to bring childhood pictures and toys.

3. Set up extra chairs for adult guests.

4. Set up a card table for the children's photos and toys.

5. Set up the Spiral Teaching Picture in the worship center.

6. Learn the songs "The Joy of the Lord" on the Resource Box cassette and "A Song of Jubilee" printed in the Student Leaflet. The complete "A Song of Jubilee" is printed in the *Jubilee Guidebook*.

●● ▽●

BIBLE STUDY FOR TEACHER ENRICHMENT

Bible Background

The writer, Luke, used Mark's Gospel account of the same story (10:13-16) as background for retelling the story of Jesus blessing the children. But unlike the writer of Mark who called the little ones "children," Luke described them as "infants" or "babes." Most of the children may have been about a year old— the age when parents took their children to receive prayers of blessing from elders or scribes. This special blessing may have occurred during the celebration of the Day of Atonement.

Whether the parents were following Jewish tradition or sensing Jesus' power and love, the disciples acted and spoke harshly. In contrast, Jesus acted lovingly toward the children. In this setting, not long before his triumphal entry to Jerusalem and his death on Golgotha, he told his listeners to become like little children.

Bible Insights

Help the children discover what qualities children have that are important for followers of Christ. For example, children are open and willing to talk. In most societies children rank lowest but demand constant attention from adults. Children are honest yet easily influenced. They are not prejudiced unless taught to be so, and they relate well to all people.

Jesus was concerned about the powerless. He taught his followers to love all people in a way that a child shows love. We should seek to take on these childlike qualities. Encourage the children to trust God, to be honest and open, and show love to others. Jesus also taught that it is possible to be *disciples* (followers) of Jesus without being strict *disciplinarians*.

Faith Nugget for Teachers

God is most concerned about the powerless. We need to become like children to receive and understand the kingdom of God.

TEACHING TIPS

Be sensitive to children from one-parent families or from non-Christian homes. Help them link up with supportive adults in the church.

When leading discussions, count silently to fifteen after posing a question. Sometimes children do not respond because we do not give them enough time. When someone does give an appropriate answer, acknowledge the idea by repeating what was said, by nodding your head, or by asking a related question.

STUDENT EXPERIENCE

Beginning Moments

1. Shake hands with children and adults as they arrive. Use a handshake appropriate to your personality and culture. Encourage the children and adults to shake hands with each other as they share greetings.

2. Direct the children and adults to a small table with name tags and pens. Instruct both children and adults to fill in the name tags with their own names and favorite early childhood toys or games. Let them pin these name tags on each other. Be sure to make introductions. Have children introduce themselves and their adult friend or relative. Or let each person say what they wrote on their name tag.

3. Let children set up a display of the photographs and toys that they brought. Spend several minutes looking at the items with the children and adults.

Bible Story

1. Anticipate the Bible story. Ask everyone to quietly move to the worship center for the Bible story. Tell the children to bring their Bibles with them. Direct the children to sit on the floor near you. Adults can sit behind their child on the floor or on chairs. After everyone is seated and quiet, pause a few moments and welcome everyone to this celebration Sunday. Say, "Today we are celebrating children. We're going to hear a story about Jesus that tells us what Jesus thought about children." Explain that in today's story, parents were bringing their one-year-olds to Jesus. In Jesus' time it was the custom in Palestine for parents to take their children to a distinguished rabbi on their first birthdays so that the rabbi could bless the children.

Before starting the story, ask the children to show the adults how we listen to the Bible story. Suggest that the children be good models so that the adults will know what to do.

2. Experience the Bible story. [*Show the Spiral Teaching Picture. Open up the box of story figures. One by one, set the people in their places and begin.*] Tell the story.

3. Wonder about the Bible story. Plan to extend the wondering time to involve children and adults. Follow the suggestions after each statement. Adapt to fit your group. Ask everyone to find Luke 18:15-17 in their Bibles. (Children can share Bibles with adults or use the text in the Student Leaflet if not all versions are the same.) Read the three verses in unison. With your Bible open in your lap, pose these questions:
• How does it feel to be a child? (Let children call out with one-word answers such as: *scary, fun, boring.*)
• How did you feel when you were a child? (Adults and children can discuss briefly in pairs and then share with the group if they wish.)
• Do you suppose it was different being a child in Jesus' time? (Children and adult pairs should talk briefly and report to group.)
• When is it fun to be a child? (Children and adults discuss in pairs then give short report to group.)
• When is it difficult? (Repeat child/adult discussions and brief group reporting.)

Responses to the Bible Story

1. Write a group letter or individual letters to the pastor or other congregational leader. Before writing, explain that because Jesus considered the children important, the church believes that children are important too. Explain that "church" does not mean only the building but rather the people of God. Hand out lined paper and pencils or pens to

everyone. Let each child and each adult compose a letter. Show a sample letter and offer suggestions of topics to be included in the letter. These might include:
• What I like about church.
• What I would like to change about my church.
• What I would be willing to do now to help my church.
• How I would like to serve the church in the future.

For a group letter use a large piece of poster board or newsprint. (A group letter will take less time if the teacher does the writing. It can provide interesting ideas if adults listen to what the children say.) Ask children to think of changes they would like to make in the church. "Sign" the letter with handprints (have finger paint ready for handprints) or thumbprints (stamp pad) and signatures. Encourage the adults to "sign" too as a way of affirming the children. Ask for one or two volunteers to hand deliver the letters at the close of Sunday school.

Closing Moments

1. Have the children say the Bible memory passage together using sign language. (See Resources, p. 92 and Student Leaflet Session 8/3.) Remind them that only two Sundays remain in the quarter.

2. Gather children and adults in adult-child pairs. Remember together how Jesus loved the children in the Bible story today. Thank Jesus for his presence in our lives. Teach the Handy Prayer Helper (Student Leaflet, p. 3) to encourage children to offer prayers that extend beyond the selfish "give me" prayers. Explain that the thumb is a reminder to pray for ourselves. The index finger reminds us to offer prayers of thanksgiving and praise to God. The middle finger reminds us to pray for all people in the world. The ring finger

BIBLE STORY

One day people were bringing their babies to Jesus because they wanted him to bless them [*Slowly move family groups toward Jesus*]. The disciples had been talking with Jesus [*Move two disciples so they see crowd. Move them between Jesus and the children*]. When they saw all the people with the little ones, they rushed [*Move disciples closer to crowd*] to the people and ordered them to go away.

"Go away. Go away," they said. "Go away. Jesus is tired. He has been preaching and teaching. He does not have time for crying babies."

But Jesus called the disciples and said, "Let the little ones come to me. Don't stop them. The kingdom of God belongs to babies like these" [*Disciples step aside*].

Jesus opened his arms to the children. They came to him, and he blessed them [*Pick up Jesus and lightly tap each child on the head*]. The children went back to their parents [*Move children to parents*]. Jesus said to everyone gathered there, "Whoever does not receive the kingdom of God as a little child will never enter it" [*Carefully place story figures back in box*].

reminds us to pray for those we love: our friends and our family members. The little finger (that points opposite the thumb) reminds us to pray for those near us. Pray silent prayers that incorporate the finger prayer helper.

3. Sing "The Joy of the Lord." (See Resource Box cassette.) Substitute the words *peace* or *love* for the word *strength* or choose other appropriate words. Teach everyone the refrain from "A Song of Jubilee" (Early Preparation #6) or let the children teach it to the adults if they remember it from last quarter.

4. Dismiss the children and adults with handshakes or hugs at the door. Be sure they take home their Student Leaflets.

CHOICES

1. Encourage the children to respond to the story in a hands-on way. Provide finger paint and glossy paper. Use two colors of dry tempera paint sprinkled on opposite ends of the paper. Add several drops of liquid starch to each area of dry paint. Retell the story and encourage the children to respond, using the finger paint. After telling the story, allow a few minutes for children to complete their pictures.

2. Have the children greet people before the worship hour. This greeting can remind adults that children are important in the worship service. Arrange for this activity ahead of time with your pastor or welcoming committee.

3. Let the children draw faces on their fingers. Children can use fine-tip markers for drawing. Then they retell the Bible story, using their finger characters. Draw Jesus on the thumb and the disciples on the other fingers of the same hand. Then draw faces of children and parents on the fingers of the other hand.

4. Telephone each parent/guardian early in the week, asking him or her to write a From-Parent-to-Child Love Note that can be handed out during class. Tell the adults to keep this note a surprise. Or let the adults write these notes while the children write letters to the pastor or church leader (Responses #1).

5. Invite a one-year-old child to class or visit the church nursery. Observe how the child depends on and trusts the adults in his or her life.

6. Make a hands-on church mural. Help your children feel a part of the church. Let them supervise the making of a church-wide mural that shows all the hands and signatures of everyone in the congregation. Talk with your pastor or church education director to plan this activity, where and when it can take place, etc. Provide commercial finger paint for full handprints or colored markers for tracing around hands.

7. Play childhood games like *Drop the Handkerchief* or *London Bridge*. Encourage the children by playing along. Allow yourself to have fun like a small child. Your example will help the older children see it is all right to be childlike. Use these games to help them remember that Christ expected all people to take on childlike qualities.

•Finger paint. Cut open the long sides of garbage bags. Tape the back and front pieces together so clothing is protected. For children who need direction, say, "Paint what it feels like to be a child," or "Paint God." Encourage children to use their fingertips rather than flat palms.

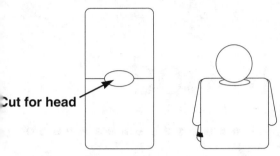

Cut for head

•Tell the Bible story. Wonder about the story.
•For Responses #1 provide crayons and let children draw what they would say about the church, using only one sentence to explain the picture.
•Sing choruses or camp songs. Choose songs you learned as a child. Let the children offer suggestions.
•Present a shadow play of the Bible story. Set up a slide projector and let children's arms and hands do the telling.
•Let the children do "Who's My Mom?" in the Student Leaflet.
•Worship together (Closing Moments).

3

TEACHING GRADE THREE

•Greet people (Choices #2). Make arrangements for children to greet people arriving for the morning worship or another church event. When explaining the activity to the children, talk with them about the importance of greeting visitors, especially guests from other countries.
•Cut out paper dolls. Fold a standard-size sheet of typing paper fan-style and cut paper dolls so arms and legs connect on the fold. Chain all the paper dolls in a large circle to represent the world.
•Tell the Bible story while a small child sits on your lap. Wonder about the story.

•Draw faces on fingers (Choices #3). Purchase a variety of colored fine-point permanent markers for children to draw faces on their fingers. Retell the story and let the children's fingers act it out, or let small groups of children dramatize the event. Challenge the children to think about what the characters would have said and to add details to make the story seem more real or modern.
•Play childhood games that the children remember playing as preschoolers (Choices #7).

4

TEACHING GRADE FOUR

•Search the Bible for babies. Challenge the children to find names of babies or children or situations where children were mentioned in the Bible.
•Read the Scripture text from the Bible. Wonder about the story.
•Ask the children to prepare a short play to present to children in the church nursery or the youngest Sunday school class. (Make arrangements ahead of time.) If possible, allow time for children to interact with the toddlers.
•Write a letter to the church (Responses #1). Use a large portion of

the class time to compose the letter to the church. If children are interested, encourage them to present their letter and ideas at a church board meeting. Counsel the recipients of the letter(s) to respond immediately to the children. (Children will expect a reply the following week!)
•Deliver From-Parent-to-Child Love Notes (Choices #4). Children this age need plenty of affirmation, especially from those they love. Plan for a secret messenger to deliver the notes.
•Worship together (Closing Moments).

5

TEACHING GRADE FIVE

What Belongs to God

TEACHER PREPARATION

Student Leaflet Answers

Memory Work Rebus: And do not set your heart on what you will eat or drink; do not worry about it. For the pagan world runs after all such things, and your Father knows that you need them (Luke 12:29-30, NIV).

Celebrate! Celebrations includes a festival for the new church school year. Plan ahead for a congregational celebration in September.

Meditation

Change me, O God of the universe. I need your all-seeing eyes to help me determine what belongs to my government and what belongs to you. Take away my confusion. Clarify my vision.

Bible Scope

Luke 20:19-26; Psalm 24:1-2

Bible Text

Luke 20:19-26

Bible Story Focus

Using a coin, Jesus taught the people to decide for themselves what belongs to God and what belongs to the government.

Bible Memory Passage

Luke 12:22-31 (29, 30)

Faith Nugget for Children

Jesus teaches us to respect both God and government.

Anticipated Outcomes

The children will recognize that everything belongs to God and that Jesus taught us to respect God and government.

Essential Supplies

• Resource Box: Spiral Teaching Picture Book, Bible Memory Poster, cassette, Bible Verse Visual

• Student Leaflets showing denarius and other coins
• Tape player
• Coins from several countries
• Spy costume: long raincoat with coin in pocket, felt dress hat, sunglasses
• 100 pennies
• Information on your country's allocation of each tax dollar
• Offering plate
• *If you use any of the Choices, gather the appropriate supplies.*

Early Preparation

1. Set up a display of coins from various countries. Ask someone who has traveled internationally, exchange students, or recent immigrants to provide the coins.

2. Obtain current information on how taxes are used by your national government. Contact the National Campaign for a Peace Tax Fund, 2121 Decatur Place N.W., Washington, DC 20008, (202) 483-3751; or Conscience Canada Inc., Box 8601, Victoria Center Post Office, Victoria, BC V8W 3S2, (604) 384-5532.

3. Prepare a large pie chart (i.e., two feet in diameter) showing how tax dollars are spent.

4. Put a coin in your pocket for the Bible story.

5. Invite someone who has refused to pay war taxes, register for the draft, or go to war to talk to your class. Ask them to tell how God has blessed them (Responses #2).

6. On the chalkboard or chart paper write these words: *taxes, government, emperor, denarius.* Allow space for adding definitions.

7. Set up the Spiral Teaching Picture in the worship center.

8. Learn the song "Take My Life and Let It Be" from the Resource Box cassette.

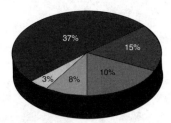

Pie chart

Bible Background

Luke used Jerusalem as the setting for this story. Earlier in the Luke account, Jesus entered the city as he rode triumphantly on the back of a colt (Luke 19:35-36). He wept over the city (v. 41) and cleansed the temple (v. 45). Chief priests, scribes, and elders questioned Jesus' authority (Luke 20:1-2), but he continued his direct teaching by telling the people "The Parable of the Wicked Tenants" (20:9). Hearing this story, the religious leaders were angry—so angry that they were ready to arrest Jesus. However, they were afraid of the people who liked him.

So the religious leaders sent their students to watch Jesus and to question his beliefs about allegiance to God and government. The religious leaders expected these students to spy on Jesus and trap him into verbalizing his allegiance to God and only God. Then the religious leaders could hand him over to the governor, and they would be rid of this Jesus who had caused problems for the temple leaders.

These spies asked if paying taxes to the emperor was in keeping with Jewish law. Jesus recognized trouble and asked to see a coin called a denarius. The choice of this coin was important. Every adult male in Judea was expected to pay an annual poll tax of one denarius (about one day's wage) to the Roman government. Although the tax was not a heavy one, most Jews hated this symbol of Roman authority over them. The issue was not political (Do we pay taxes to the government?) but religious (Is it wrong to pay tribute to anyone besides God?).

Jesus surprised his listeners with his answer. He told them to give to both God and Caesar. The spies sent by the religious leaders were amazed by this answer and silenced.

Bible Insights

Few people in history have liked paying taxes. The issue of taxation, however, is not the important point of the Scripture passage.

The issue focuses on authority. To whose authority do we bow? What belongs to whom? As you teach, help the children to understand respect for both God and government. Issues of taxes and authority can become complex. Children will understand that it takes money to make a church and a government run effectively. Help them understand that we are first of all under God's authority.

Faith Nugget for Teachers

Since the entire world belongs to God, our ultimate allegiance belongs to God.

BIBLE STUDY FOR TEACHER ENRICHMENT

STUDENT EXPERIENCE

Beginning Moments

1. Wear a spy costume to greet children at the door or in the hallway. Whisper "I'm being sent on a secret mission" to each person who comes to the door.

2. Direct the children to the display of international money. Point out coins that show a person's head and talk about what designs are featured on the coins and bills. Let the children handle the coins and talk about them.

3. Listen to individual children recite the memory passage while children look at the money. Gather as a group and recite the memory passage antiphonally by verses.

Bible Story

1. Anticipate the Bible story. Ask children to direct their attention to the chalkboard on which you wrote these words: *taxes, government, emperor, denarius.* Ask the children to give meanings for these words. Possible definitions are:

taxes—a certain amount of money that those in charge of a government require all people to pay;

government—the group of people who makes decisions for all people who live in a country;

emperor—the highest ruler of a country, like a king (Caesar was the emperor of the Roman Empire when Jesus lived);

denarius—a small silver coin of ancient Rome.

Show the Student Leaflet picture of a denarius. Explain to the children that this coin is mentioned in our story.

Using a stage whisper, explain that there are spies in today's story. Remind the children to listen closely and not to talk while you tell the story.

2. Experience the Bible story. Direct the children to sit on the floor as you prepare to tell the story [*Point to the Spiral Teaching Picture*]. Tell the story.

3. Wonder about the Bible story. Continue in a quiet, reflective mood. Offer these wondering statements:

•I wonder how the spies felt before they tried to trick Jesus and after Jesus answered them.

•I wonder if the spies continued spying on Jesus.

•I wonder if any of the spies changed after talking with Jesus.

•I wonder what Jesus meant when he said, "Give to the emperor the things that are the emperor's, and give to God the things that are God's." Are there some taxes that are wrong? Are there some times when we should not respect government leaders?

•I wonder which character in the story I am most like—the spies, Jesus' disciples and friends.

Encourage the children to ask questions or respond with their ideas. Value their comments.

Responses to the Bible Story

1. Let children choose. After explaining the two choices, call each child by name and ask what he or she would like to do. Children can work alone, in small groups, or in large groups. Let them do the organizing to carry out the activity.

a. Act out the story. Children determine how the story will be retold. Possibilities might include puppets, play, readers' theater, story figures, or song.

b. Count pennies to stack in areas of a pie chart. (Use the information from Early Preparation #2.) One penny can represent each dollar. Explain to the children that for each dollar that their families pay to the government in taxes, the money is divided to pay for different things. After arranging pennies for each area of the graph, the children will have questions. Encourage discus-

sion or ask questions like these:
• Which areas receive the most/least tax money?
• Which areas should receive more or less tax money?

Allow time for both groups of children to share with each other.

2. Prepare the children for the guest speaker. Lead a short discussion and help them make a list of some questions to ask the guest. For example: Why did you choose not to register for the armed forces (go to war, or pay war taxes)? Who helped you make this decision? How did this decision affect your life? Who supported you in this decision?

Let your guest tell a personal story of how God blessed his or her life through this decision.

Closing Moments

1. Worship together while the guest is still with you. (a) Sing "Take My Life and Let It Be." (See Resource Box cassette.) (b) Pray together. Kneel around your guest. Invite the children to repeat each phrase and action after you.

Dear God [*Look up, hands clasped in prayer*],

I offer you my praise [*Hands to mouth, then arms and hands stretched upwards*].

I offer you my heart [*Hands crossed over chest, then stretched upwards*].

I offer you my money [*One hand lifts pretend money from open palm of other hand, then stretched upwards*].

I offer you my life [*Head down, hands at sides, arms lift up and stretch upwards, head rises and eyes look up*].

Thank you for everything you give to me [*Eyes up, hands meet above head, fingers extended*].

Amen [*Head bows, hands are lowered and clasped at elbow level*].

Text from *Hymnal: A Worship Book*, #748, 1992, Hymnal Project. Used by permission.

BIBLE STORY

[*Stage whisper*] I *was* a spy. One day I was called to meet with the leaders of the Jews. There were other spies there too. The scribes and chief priests gave us spies a very important assignment. They told us to find a man named Jesus—Jesus from Galilee—and to follow this man. We were to pretend to be very honest and even to compliment him on his good works. Then we were supposed to get him to say something that could get him into big trouble with the authorities in the government.

The other spies and I set out to find this Jesus. He was fairly easy to spot because wherever he went, a crowd gathered to talk with him and to listen to his stories. Our job was to trap Jesus into saying something that would get him arrested. When the moment came, I was the one who did the talking.

[*Full voice*] "Teacher," I asked, "we know that you are right in what you say and teach, and we know that you bow to no one here on earth but teach the way of God as truth."

[*Stage whisper*] I had the attention of Jesus and the attention of everyone around. All eyes were on me. I swallowed, took a breath, and asked the big question. [*Full voice*] "Is it lawful for us to pay taxes to the emperor, or not?"

[*Stage whisper*] I could hear whispering among the people behind me. I could see the other spies edging in closer to hear Jesus' answer. Then Jesus spoke.

[*Jesus' voice*] "Show me a denarius," he said.

[*Stage whisper*] I searched in my clothing for a denarius—the coin with Caesar's picture on it [*Find a coin in your pocket and hold it up*]. I gave the coin to Jesus.

[*Jesus' voice*] "Whose head and whose title are on it?" Jesus asked as he held the coin up high.

[*Full voice*] "The emperor's," I said. [*Stage whisper*] I wondered what he was getting at.

[*Jesus' voice*] "Then give to the emperor the things that are the emperor's, and give to God the things that are God's."

[*Stage whisper*] I looked at the other spies. One of them shrugged his shoulders, telling me he didn't know what else to say. All of us were amazed by Jesus' answer, and all of us were silent as we moved away.

2. As you dismiss the children with a word of blessing, remind them that next Sunday is the last session together during the quarter, and that you will review the Bible stories you have studied. Be sure they take home their Student Leaflets.

CHOICES

1. Prepare the children for the guest speaker you have asked to talk about giving in church or Sunday school. If possible, meet the person where the money is collected, counted, or recorded. Make arrangements for this ahead of time. Before you go, discuss questions the children may wish to ask. Remind the children to listen closely and to respect the speaker. Questions may include the following:
• Who decides how the offering money is used?
• Who counts the money?
• Who sends the money to the different organizations that get the money?
• How much money is needed each year to maintain the church building?
• Why do we have offerings?

2. Make a pie chart that shows how your church giving is used. The children can gather information, prepare a chart (with help), and color sections of the chart. This could be made available to the congregation.

3. Count the church or Sunday school offering for the church treasurer.

4. Write letters or postcards to state or provincial representatives of the national government. Encourage these representatives to allow people to follow their conscience or mention specific legislation that addresses how the taxes are spent.

5. Sing "Seek Ye First the Kingdom." (See Resource Box cassette.)

6. Using the international coins, design posters that children can take home to remind them about giving. Have the children find Luke 20:25 and copy the words in large letters on the poster. They can make drawings of the coins to decorate the poster.

**Student Leaflet
Puzzling Words Key**

Fill in the boxes. Put the correct letters from the puzzle in each box.

1 G	2 i	3 v	4 e	5	6 t	7 o	8	9 C	10 a
11 e	12 s	13 a	14 r	15	16 w	17 h	18 a	19 t	20
21 i	22 s	23	24 C	25 a	26 e	27 s	28 a	29 r	30 '
31 s	32	33 a	34 n	35 d	36	37 t	38 o	39	40 G
41 o	42 d	43	44 w	45 h	46 a	47 t	48	49 i	50 s
51	52 G	53 o	54 d	55 '	56 s	57	58 L	59 u	60 k
61 e	62	63 2	64 0	65 :	66 2	67 5			

- Wear a Bible costume. Or ask a child to wear a traditional Bible costume to greet the children at the door.
- Clap the Bible memory passage. Present the Bible memory using a simple clapping pattern to help children remember important words.
- Explain the meanings of words: *spies, taxes, government, emperor, denarius, authorities.*
- Tell the Bible story. Be the spy. Wonder about the story.

- Let the children hunt for treasure. Hide clues inside and outside the church building that lead children to the offering plate and guest speaker (Choices #1). For added difficulty, have the children look up Bible verses to answer clues.
- Listen to the speaker.
- Worship together around the offering plate.
- Work on activities in the Student Leaflet. Let children choose activities.

3
TEACHING GRADE THREE

- Look at international coins.
- Read about money. Use the Student Leaflet or library books.
- Introduce vocabulary words.
- Read the Bible story directly from the Bible.
- Wonder about the story. For large classes let children write down their wondering questions for you to read.
- Have the children draw lots for Response options. To facilitate decision making, write options on slips of paper and let children draw choices out of an

old purse or wallet. They can trade or draw again until they get an option they like. Options are: (a) draw Luke 20:25 posters; (b) count pennies (Response #2); (c) make an audio cassette tape that encourages freedom of conscience. Send it to a government representative.
- Sing "Seek Ye First the Kingdom of God" during Closing Moments. Pray together, asking for guidance in respecting God and government.

4
TEACHING GRADE FOUR

- Be a spy. Ask another adult to represent Jesus. Present the story in dialogue form.
- Hand out small notebooks and pencils. Tell children to record their questions as the Bible story is being presented.
- Act out the Bible story with the other adult. Wonder about the story.
- Have children imagine they are newspaper reporters. Set up a press conference and let them ask both of you questions.
- Write for the *Jerusalem Times.* Children work in small groups to write news articles for the newspaper in the

Student Leaflet. Plan to publish these articles in the church bulletin or newsletter.
- Talk about government spending and areas of government that children feel need greater or less funding.
- Design "What belongs to Caesar, what belongs to God" campaign buttons that can be sent to government representatives as a reminder to spend money wisely.
- Worship together, inviting children to offer their hearts and their money to God's service.

5
TEACHING GRADE FIVE

13 True Greatness

TEACHER PREPARATION

Student Leaflet Answers

Servings of Scripture: (1) c; (2) b; (3) j; (4) g; (5) d; (6) h; (7) i; (8) f; (9) e; (10) a.

Scripture Swirl: 1 cup brown sugar, ⅓ cup milk, ¼ cup light corn syrup, 1 tablespoon butter, ¼ cup peanut butter, chopped nuts.

Meditation

Great God, lift me to a new understanding of service as I teach this lesson. Fill me with the air of your Spirit and prepare me to serve your children with unfailing willingness.

Bible Scope

Luke 22:1-30

Bible Text

Luke 22:24-30

Bible Story Focus

When the disciples argued about who was greater, Jesus demonstrated that greatness comes through serving others.

Bible Memory Passage

Luke 12:22-31 (31)

Faith Nugget for Children

Greatness comes in serving others.

Anticipated Outcomes

The children will understand Jesus' teachings about greatness and develop an attitude of service.

Essential Supplies

•Resource Box: Spiral Teaching Picture Book, cassette, Bible Memory Visual

•Student Leaflets
•Tape player
•Story figures—entire set from general classroom items (Get several extra figures if possible.)
•Three boards (3 x 8 x 2 in., 7.5 x 20 x 5 cm.) and pieces of cloth for storytelling
•Picnic basket with snack supplies and tableware for everyone
•Small catapult (old serving spoon, large eraser), cotton balls, tape measure
•Pencils and small pieces of paper
•Coffee mug
•*If you use any of the Choices, gather the appropriate supplies.*

Early Preparation

1. Set up three rectangular tables in a U-shape (see illustration), if classroom space allows.

2. Draw a diagram of the table on the board.

3. On the floor set up a small catapult using a serving spoon and an eraser. Have cotton balls and tape measure nearby.

4. Write key words from the Bible memory passage on slips of paper (one word per paper). Place them in a coffee mug.

5. Put the picnic basket and supplies near the door. Set plates for each child on the table. Have extras available for guests.

6. Set up the Spiral Teaching Picture in the worship center.

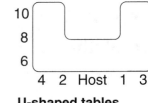

U-shaped tables

● ● ▽ ●

Bible Background

The setting for Luke's account of the disciples' dispute about greatness differed from the accounts in Matthew 20:20-28 and Mark 10:35-45. Matthew attributed the request to the mother of James and John. Mark had these two disciples appealing to Jesus for prestigious places in heaven. Both writers placed the action prior to Jesus' triumphal entry into Jerusalem.

Luke, however, included this story during the Lord's Supper. Placing the story in this context added a certain poignancy to the dispute between the disciples as they argued about each one's importance at a time when Jesus was sharing his final meal with them. The dispute as told by Luke related to the Jewish custom of seating at festival meals.

The Jews had definite seating arrangements at feasts. Tables were arranged with the host in the center and the most important guest to the right of the host. On the host's left sat the second most important guest. Seating continued like this around the table. (See illustration.)

Jesus confronted the dispute directly. He told the disciples that servanthood, not power, best defined the kingdom that he was trying to offer them. In using the word *benefactor*, Jesus referred to the Greek monarchs who had ruled over Egypt and Syria. Jesus challenged leaders to demonstrate humble service and used himself as the example of "one who serves."

Bible Insights

Help the class understand the concept of servanthood, one of Jesus' important teachings that is central to our Anabaptist and Friends beliefs. Challenge the children to recognize how serving others contrasts with the prevalent secular idea that winning and being first or best are everything. Encourage the children to apply Jesus' teaching to their everyday living.

Faith Nugget for Teachers

Service is the road to greatness.

BIBLE STUDY FOR TEACHER ENRICHMENT

TEACHING TIPS

Be sensitive to your group when you plan the activity in Beginning Moments #2. Any kind of competitive game will work, but try to choose one that will not have an obvious loser. Lighten the tension with a joke.

To learn to know your children, share a meal with individuals or small groups outside of class time. Sit together at church fellowship meals, invite small groups to your home, or eat at a restaurant.

STUDENT EXPERIENCE

Beginning Moments

1. Greet the children as they arrive. Connect with their activities during the week.

Explain to the children that the tables need to be set for the snack you will have later. From the picnic basket next to the door, let children choose items of tableware. Ask them to add flatware, glasses, and napkins next to the plates that you have set on the tables.

2. Direct the children to the catapult you have set up. Present the children with cotton balls and challenge them to see who can shoot the cotton ball the farthest. Inform the children that you will award a prize to the one who is the greatest catapult shooter. Allow several minutes for the children to compete. Provide a tape measure to record length of shots. When all the children have had several tries, award a small prize to the person with the *shortest* shot. As the children argue among themselves and complain to you, explain that they sound just like Jesus' disciples in today's story.

Bible Story

1. Anticipate the Bible story. Direct the children to sit on the floor near the worship center. After they are seated, explain that at Jewish feasts, like the one in the story for today, the seating arrangement was very important. Point out the table diagram on the board. Explain where the host would sit and where the guests would sit in order of importance (see Bible Background). Servants would serve the meal that could last for several hours. Guests would recline on couches around three sides of a U-shaped or square table.

Explain that this discussion between the disciples occurred right after the Lord's Supper (Last Supper). Jesus hosted this last meal with his disciples.

2. Experience the Bible story. [*In the worship center arrange three boards (see Essential Supplies) in U shape to represent dinner table. Cover with pieces of cloth. Have the story figures handy. Be sure the Spiral Teaching Picture is nearby.*] Tell the story.

3. Wonder about the Bible story. Look briefly at the Spiral Teaching Picture. Then offer these wondering thoughts to stimulate questions or discussion:
•I wonder how this argument started.
•I wonder how the disciples felt when they were arguing and how they felt when Jesus talked to them.
•I wonder what kinds of things we argue about. Do you ever argue about where to sit at the table or in the car or on the bus? Is arguing different from disagreeing?
•I wonder how a real servant acts.
•I wonder what it means to be number one (greatest) in God's kingdom. Is it okay to be number one at anything?

Discuss questions the children may have. If the children have questions about the passage, instruct them to find and read the text in their Bibles.

Responses to the Bible Story

1. Listen to the cassette recording of "Let Me Be Your Servant, Jesus." Pass out the Student Leaflets. Sing the song together.

2. After singing, join hands around the table, elbows on the table and hands held up. As you say the following prayer, have the children repeat the lines after you. Before you begin, tell them the last line is "Amen."

Number one God
When we argue
When we boast
About who's number one,
Help us, God,
To remember

That you're number one
And we are your servants
Together.
Amen.

3. Invite the children to think of ways they serve other people at home, at school, in the community, or in the world. Hand out pencils and small pieces of paper to each child. Let them work on the floor or wherever they can find space. Ask them to answer this question. How do you serve others? Have them write or draw their ideas—each on a separate paper.

Encourage many ideas. To get their thinking started, ask them to think of ways that grown-ups help others.

Allow each child one or two opportunities to mime an action of service. Let the other children guess what is being portrayed.

4. Encourage children to initiate ideas of a service that would help others in the congregation, community, or world. Sit on the floor to plan a class service event. Consider making this an anonymous activity where the recipient would not know who the servants were.

5. Use a Word Cup to review the quarter's Bible memory (Early Preparation #4). Let each child select from a coffee mug a slip of paper that has a key word from one of the verses. Children take turns reading their words. The children try to recite the verse together.

Closing Moments

1. Invite the children to sit at the table they helped set earlier. Let them serve each other a snack you have prepared. Let the serving take on the flavor of a ritual. When the children serve someone, ask them to repeat the words "Let me be your servant, (name of child being served)." Practice saying this together several times.

BIBLE STORY

On the night when Jesus had gathered his disciples for a final meal together, Jesus sat where the host would usually sit [*Set Jesus figure in place*]. The disciples were all seated around the table [*Put disciples in place, giving each a number*]. The servants served the meal [*Each servant enters, touches table, and stands in place*].

After the meal the disciples started arguing about who was the number one disciple.

"I'm the best," said one of them [*Point to disciple 1*].

"No, I am" [*Point to disciple 2*].

"Peter is" [*Point to disciple 7*].

"No, John is" [*Point to disciple 10*].

Everyone was arguing [*Pause*] except Jesus [*Point to Jesus*].

"In the world," said Jesus, "among people who do not follow me, there are powerful rulers. That is not my way. The one who is number one must become like the last. The real leader is the one who serves. I am here to be a servant to all."

The argument was over, and everyone remembered Jesus' words.

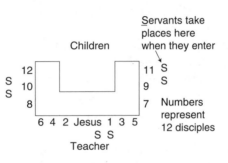

2. Explain to the children that this session ends the quarter's activities. Thank them for their participation. Offer a prayer of blessing as you dismiss each one. Be sure they take home their Student Leaflets and any items they may have made during the quarter.

CHOICES

Use these ideas in place of or to supplement the session plan.

1. Invite a panel of church members of various ages to answer questions about acts of service they have performed. This activity will help children understand what kinds of long- or short-term service opportunities are available and how service can be a lifetime calling. Select individuals who represent a wide range of church service experiences.

2. Make a collage of clippings about service activities. Search through church periodicals, including those from your own congregation or conference, for articles, photos, and headlines about service activities. Use these clippings to make a collage that can be displayed for the congregation to see. One effective way to mount the clippings would be to cut the letters S-E-R-V-E out of poster board and mount the clippings on these letters, cutting edges even with sides of the letters.

3. Show children a table tennis ball and paddle and ask them to explain how these are related to the session's theme. Answer: In table tennis one team serves the ball to another. It is impossible to play the game without giving up the ball to the other team. That is the way our Christian lives are. In order to live as Christ taught, we must give our lives in service to other people.

When you dismiss the children, hand out table tennis balls on which you have written: "Serve God." Challenge children to do an act of service whenever they see this ball. (Use a sport common to most children in your church: volleyball, racquetball, tennis, badminton, handball. Instead of handing out table tennis balls, draw balls on construction paper and cut them out.)

4. Pose a picture of the Lord's Supper. Use the famous Leonardo da Vinci painting or a picture of a black Jesus with his disciples to foster ideas. Let one or two children arrange other children to form a still-life picture of the Bible story. Have children title the picture and use a camera to photograph it for possible use by the congregation.

5. Review the quarter with balloons. For classes with regular attendance, use this activity to recall the quarter's Bible stories. On small pieces of paper, write questions from all lessons. Fold up the papers and slip them inside balloons (one per balloon); then blow up the balloons and tie. Tape the balloons to the table. Each child gets a chance to pop a balloon with a push pin and read the question for the entire class to answer.

6. Play the *ACTS* game. (See Resource Box and Teacher's Guide Resources, p. 92.) Write questions that help the children review the stories from this quarter.

- Set the table for the snack.
- Invite another class to be guests at the end of class. (Make arrangements ahead of time.)
- Tell the story. Use the story figures for people and small pieces of cardboard to represent the tables.
- Find the story in Luke 22:24-30. Reread it aloud verse by verse.
- Sing "Let Me Be Your Servant, Jesus" and other songs related to service.
- Share a time of worship. Light the candles on the Lenten Candle Cross Mat used during the Easter sessions. Say, "Just as Jesus came to earth to serve, let us go out to serve all people on earth."
- Read a picture book related to the service theme, or tell a story about a church member's experience in a service-related event.
- Encourage the children to mime actions of service.
- Let the children serve a snack to guests.
- Review the quarter by having the children complete "Servings of Scripture" in the Student Leaflet.

3
TEACHING GRADE THREE

- Prepare "Scripture Swirl" (recipe in Student Leaflet) in the church kitchen. Allow it to cool during class time.
- See the story. Have adults from the congregation act out the Bible story in your classroom. The children return from kitchen to discover the actors arguing about who will sit in which seat. Wonder about the Bible story.
- Choose service. Have the children make collages with cutouts from church periodicals or write letters to long- or short-term volunteers.
- Let the children pop balloons. Use slips of paper inside balloons to review the quarter's lessons or Bible memory.
- Eat "Scripture Swirls." Share with the children that the result of true service is a sweet mixture of unexpected blessings.

4
TEACHING GRADE FOUR

- Have the children toss cotton balls. Determine who is the greatest by the shortest, not the longest, throw (Beginning Moments #2). Talk about how our society measures greatness.
- Listen to the Bible story. Have one or two of your children prepare and tell the story.
- Wonder about the story. Discuss "Which One Is Greater?" from the Student Leaflet.
- Learn about service experiences. Listen to a panel of church members talk about church service experiences, either as givers or recipients. Allow time for children to ask questions. Provide maps to show the class where these members served.
- Serve a snack to your guests. Let the children do the serving.
- Review the quarter. Hold up the Spiral Teaching Pictures from the quarter and let children tell you the stories.
- Help the church custodian. Plan a class service event to help the custodian clean the church. Present a work list and a note to parents detailing date and time.
- Relate table tennis game to service (Choices #3).

5
TEACHING GRADE FIVE

Resources

Clip Art

Instructions: Use the clip art scattered throughout these Resource Pages to decorate your notes or letters to parents and children. The numbers represent the sessions to which they relate.

Bulletin Board Ideas

Use these ideas for bulletin boards, walls, or to decorate your door.

Write the names of your children on the puzzle pieces, hands, and feet, or let children decorate and write their names on these items. Let them put the puzzle together as a cooperative project.

5. & 7.

We Need Each Piece To Be Complete

Let Us Be Your Servants, Jesus

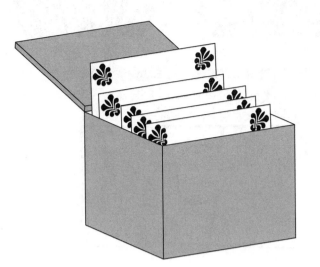

Consequence Box

Copy this page and cut the cards apart. Make more cards with other consequences you think are important.

If a child chooses to disregard a class rule, consequences must be paid. The child is asked to take the first consequence card in the box and write a response on paper. Direct the child to leave the room to work on these questions and to return when finished. For those not able to read or write, these consequences can be done verbally or with drawings.

The Bible says, "Blessed are the peacemakers." What is a peacemaker? Write two sentences that tell how you have been a peacemaker.	What three important things would you tell a friend about Jesus?	Think of a person who loves you. Write down that person's name. Write three sentences about how that person shows love to you.
Think of a time you helped a friend. Tell what you did and how you felt.	Write three important rules every classroom should have. Tell how you will follow these rules.	List three ways you can show respect for others. Write a sentence about how you show respect for others.
Jesus said, "Love one another as I have loved you." How do you show people you love them?	The Golden Rule is "Do unto others as you would have them do unto you." What does this mean? Write an example of how you follow this rule.	Who is your best friend? Why do you like the person? Why does she or he like you?
Think of a person you know who does good things for others. Who is this person and what does he or she do? How would you like to be like that person?	Christians take time to be kind to one another. Tell about a time when you were kind to someone who wasn't your best friend.	Write three things you like about yourself. What do you like best?

Bird Pattern
Session 7

Use this pattern to create the DO NOT WORRY BIRD. Fold a 12 x 18 in., 30 x 45 cm., piece of construction paper. Lay bird on fold, trace it, and cut out.

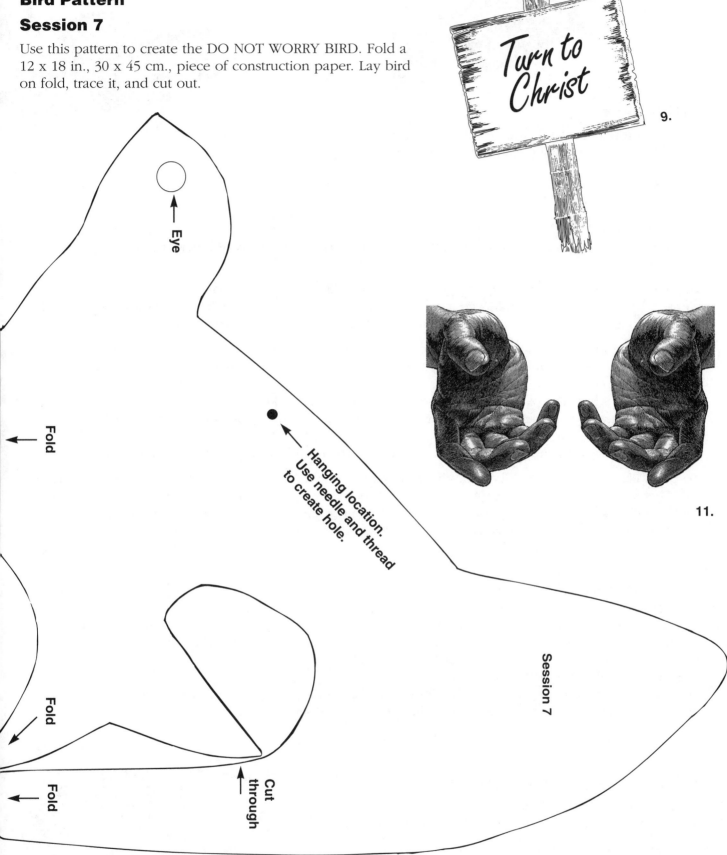

← Eye

Fold →

●
Hanging location.
Use needle and thread
to create hole.

Fold ↙

Fold →

Cut
through ↑

Session 7

Turn to Christ

9.

11.

5.

4.

ACTS game

(For use throughout the quarter. Prepare the game pieces for the Resource Box.)
A game of **A**ction, **C**oloring, and **T**ruthful **S**peech

Directions:
For two or more players

Supplies needed: ACTS playing cards from the Resource Box, colored markers, dry erase board and eraser (or other drawing equipment appropriate for group size), Bible dictionary, teacher's questions (see ACTS CARDS).

Before playing: Decide on your own rules. How long will you play? Will you play competitively or non-competitively? Will players be allowed to use a Bible dictionary or ask for help if words are unfamiliar? Do you need a judge or scorekeeper? Will you limit the time each player can use to plan a presentation?

How to play: In turn, each player draws a card from the top of the pile, selects one of the three words (phrases or events), and tries to get other players to say the word. The player must use one of the following ways:
1. Act out the word. The player may not speak while performing the word.
2. Color or draw pictures representing the word. The player may not speak and may not write words or numbers.
3. Speak without using the word or any form of the word. The player may not use actions while speaking.

To play: Player 1 draws a card, decides how to present the word, announces the category (Old Testament, New Testament, Today) and presents the word. Subsequent players continue as Player 1. However, they *must* select a different form of presentation than the player immediately preceding. For example, if Player 1 has drawn pictures, Player 2 must act or speak. If player 2 chooses to speak, Player 3 must act or draw, and so on. The object of the game is to have fun with Bible words and phrases. If you are not having fun, stop playing!

***ACTS* Cards:** On each *ACTS* card are three words, phrases, or sentences. OT means the word is from the Old Testament. NT means the word is from the New Testament. TODAY means the word is from life among today's Christians. Prior to play, the teacher/leader writes and numbers twenty names, places, or events within the life of your faith community. These are handed to players when they draw cards that have specific numbers (for example, Teacher Question #1).
IT'S TIME TO BEGIN PLAY. Lights, Camera, ACTSion!
Suggestions: For long or difficult words, present small parts at a time. Tug on your ear (or draw a picture of an ear) to indicate a word that sounds like the one you have selected.

Bible Memory Sign Language

(Sessions 8, see Student Leaflet)
Who of you by worrying can add a single hour to [your] life?

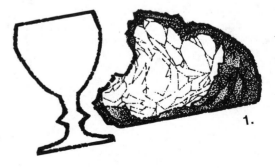

1.

String Trick Story

String was used in an ancient method of storytelling. The storyteller would use loops of string to capture the attention of the audience and make the story come alive.

How to do the *String Trick:*

Step 1: Hang the string loop over the fingers and thumb of your left hand.

Step 2: Put your right hand into the hanging loop. Use your right index finger like a hook to take hold of the string that crosses between your left thumb and index finger. With your right index finger, pull out a short loop in this string. Pull the loop out <u>under</u> the string that hangs over your left thumb. Keep the loop straight.

Step 3: Hold this loop with your right index finger and thumb and give it half a twist clockwise. Put this loop on your left index finger and pull on the hanging loop to lighten the strings. (This process will be repeated on the rest of your fingers. Keep one string across your palm and one hanging down the back. Continue to use the right index finger as a hook, working under the string that hangs across your palm. Don't forget to add the twist each time.)

Step 4: Pull out a loop in the back string between your index finger and middle finger. As before, pull it out under the string that hangs across your palm, give it half a twist clockwise, and put it on your middle finger. Tighten the strings.

Step 5: Pull out a loop between your middle finger and fourth finger, give it half a twist clockwise, and put it on your fourth finger. Tighten the strings.

Step 6: Pull out a loop between your fourth finger and little finger, give it half a twist clockwise, and put it on your little finger. Tighten the strings.

Step 7: Take the loop off your thumb. Pull the front string of the hanging loop.

26 Ways to Use Drama in Teaching the Bible, Judy Gattis Smith. Copyright 1988 by Abingdon Press. Adapted by permission.

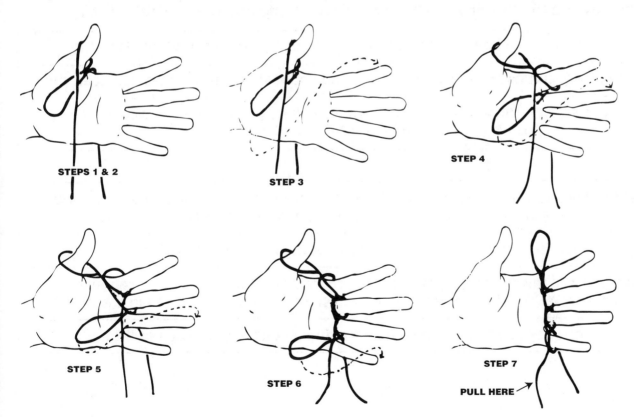

STEPS 1 & 2

STEP 3

STEP 4

STEP 5

STEP 6

STEP 7

PULL HERE

Teacher: Select the Bible translation you are learning in class. Make copies for individuals or small groups. Cut strips apart. Have the children put them in the correct order.

Do Not Worry

Then Jesus said to his disciples: "Therefore I tell you, do not worry about your life, what you will eat; or about your body, what you will wear.

Life is more than food, and the body more than clothes.

Consider the ravens: They do not sow or reap, they have no storeroom or barn; yet God feeds them. And how much more valuable you are than birds!

Who of you by worrying can add a single hour to his life?

Since you cannot do this very little thing, why do you worry about the rest?

Consider how the lilies grow. They do not labor or spin. Yet I tell you, not even Solomon in all his splendor was dressed like one of these.

If that is how God clothes the grass of the field, which is here today, and tomorrow is thrown into the fire, how much more will he clothe you, O you of little faith!

And do not set your heart on what you will eat or drink; do not worry about it.

For the pagan world runs after all such things, and your Father knows that you need them.

But seek his kingdom, and these things will be given to you as well."
Luke 12:22-31, New International Version (NIV)

He said to his disciples, "Therefore I tell you, do not worry about your life, what you will eat, or about your body, what you will wear.

For life is more than food, and the body more than clothing.

Consider the ravens: they neither sow nor reap, they have neither storehouse nor barn, and yet God feeds them. Of how much more value are you than the birds!

And can any of you by worrying add a single hour to your span of life?

If then you are not able to do so small a thing as that, why do you worry about the rest?
Consider the lilies, how they grow: they neither toil nor spin; yet I tell you, even Solomon in all his glory was not clothed like one of these.
But if God so clothes the grass of the field, which is alive today and tomorrow is thrown into the oven, how much more will he clothe you—you of little faith!
And do not keep striving for what you are to eat and what you are to drink, and do not keep worrying.
For it is the nations of the world that strive after all these things, and your Father knows that you need them.
Instead, strive for his kingdom, and these things will be given to you as well." Luke 12:22-31, New Revised Standard Version (NRSV)

Music used in this quarter

Resource Box (Cassette):

1. "Let Us Break Bread Together," *Hymnal: A Worship Book* #453
2. "Were You There," *Hymnal: A Worship Book* #257
3. "Christ the Lord Is Risen Today," *Hymnal: A Worship Book* #280
4. "Seek Ye First the Kingdom of God," *Hymnal: A Worship Book* #324
5. "Wash Me"
6. "Do Not Worry"
7. "The Wedding Banquet"
8. "The Joy of the Lord Is My Strength"
9. "Take My Life," *Hymnal: A Worship Book* #389
10. "Let Me Be Your Servant, Jesus"
11. "Asithi: Amen," *Hymnal: A Worship Book* #64

Resource Box (Song Chart):

1: "Wash Me"
2. "Do Not Worry"

Student Leaflet:

Session 1: "Let Us Break Bread Together"
Session 4: "You Shall Go Out with Joy"
Session 5: "Seek Ye First the Kingdom of God"
Session 6: "Wash Me"
Session 7: "Do Not Worry"
Session 8: "Asithi: Amen"
Session 11: "A Song of Jubilee"
Session 13: "Let Me Be Your Servant, Jesus"

Bibliography

Mackowski, Richard M. *Jerusalem City of Jesus.* Grand Rapids, Michigan: William B. Erdmans Publishing Co., 1980.

Millard, Alan. *Discoveries for the Time of Jesus.* Batavia, Illinois: Lion Publishing Corp., 1990.

Parker, Marjorie Hodgson. *Jellyfish Can't Swim and Other Secrets from the Animal World.* Elgin, Illinois, and Weston, Ontario: David C. Cook Publishing Co., 1991.

Smith, Judy Gattis. *26 Ways to Use Drama in Teaching the Bible.* Nashville: Abingdon Press, 1988.

Sternberg, Martin L. A. *American Sign Language: A Comprehensive Dictionary.* New York: Harper and Row Publishers, 1981.

Zohary, Michael. *Plants of the Bible.* New York: Cambridge University Press, 1982.

• •

WHAT DO YOU THINK?

Please complete this evaluation **within a month** after teaching the course of study. Copy the form, complete it, and send it to the address listed below. All denominational curriculum efforts will benefit from your feedback.

Denomination:

☐ Brethren in Christ   ☐ Church of the Brethren   ☐ Friends United Meeting

☐ General Conference Mennonite ☐ Mennonite Brethren   ☐ Mennonite Church

☐ Other_____

City _____State/Province _____

Evaluator (optional) _____

Circle correct information:

Cycle:	Quarter:	Level:	Grades Taught:			
A	Fall	Early Childhood	*Ages*	2	3	4
B	Winter	Primary	*Grades*	K	1	2
C	Spring	Middler		3	4	5
	Summer	Junior Youth		6	7	8

Name of Course:_____

Jubilee Evaluation (check one)

	Agree		Disagree	
	1	**2**	**3**	**4**
1. The theology was good.	☐	☐	☐	☐
Comment:_____				
2. The methods were creative.	☐	☐	☐	☐
Comment:_____				
3. I liked the suggested story method.	☐	☐	☐	☐
Comment:_____				
4. I found the materials appropriate for my class.	☐	☐	☐	☐
Comment:_____				
5. I found the Teacher's Guide easy to use.	☐	☐	☐	☐
Comment:_____				
6. The experiences were meaningful to the children.	☐	☐	☐	☐
Comment:_____				
7. The children liked the student pieces.	☐	☐	☐	☐
Comment:_____				
8. Resource Box materials were helpful.	☐	☐	☐	☐
Comment:_____				

9. What did you like about the curriculum? _____

_____

10. Suggestions for the future: _____

Send to Jubilee Project Office, Box 347, Newton KS 67114-0347